How Ally Found Her Financial Freedom

Dora DeLellis

ISBN: 978-0-9974244-0-9

TABLE OF CONTENTS

NOW

Ally woke up on Saturday morning just as the sun came through her bedroom window. She felt well rested and rolled over with a relaxing exhale. It had been a rough week and it was nice to know she didn't have to rush off anywhere. Better yet, she had the whole day to herself. It was a beautiful spring day with a perfectly clear sky and she intended to enjoy the nice weather. *Maybe I'll go to the park and just walk around. Grab lunch and an ice cream on the way back.*

Her agenda for today was simple. She had one online bill to pay. Not only was it the only thing on her to-do list, but she had set aside the money well in advance to pay her obligation.

Ally's mind drifted to her other financial accomplishments. She was three months ahead of her rent, her renter's insurance was paid in full, and her employee 401(k) contribution percentage was the highest it had ever been. Her savings account was up. Her credit card balance was down—by almost half of what it was one year ago.

After she paid her bill, she decided to check her bank balance. Wow. She had more than three thousand dollars saved. It was great to know that she had a good cushion and was not behind on any bills. She was also three paychecks ahead of her rent payment. After her next paycheck, she was going to transfer a little more money from her checking to her savings account.

What a difference a year makes! A year ago, she felt miscast in her own life, with money issues always hanging over her head. She was behind on her credit card payments, paying late fees, and wishing she had money in the bank. She tried to be oblivious to it all and let life happen, but it hindered her ability to think clearly. Ultimately, it all came crashing down until she realized it was time to do something about it. It had seemed like a mystery back then, a jigsaw puzzle missing pieces, or a Rubik's cube where the color platform constantly changed. She couldn't understand how people managed all their expenses and still got ahead. At this time last year, it seemed like such a tall order and she had been afraid it couldn't be done.

Now, everything felt better. The bed felt cushier and the comforter more comforting.

It had been a year of information gathering and simple planning. It required a little bit of discipline but it wasn't rocket science. All the reading was informational and interesting. It was also not as difficult as she thought it would be.

It felt so much better to be in control of her finances, and not the other way around. Armed with knowledge and insight, her confidence level had soared. She hadn't even been aware of the full impact the stress was having on her well-being. Once she had achieved financial stability, it felt as if a barbell had been lifted off her back and she could breathe easier. Now she could make financial decisions *before* a crisis without having to postpone her goals.

The credit card bill that she had just paid online was for planned spending, not reckless spending. Everything on that credit card bill was for necessary or anticipated expenses for which Ally had saved in advance.

She was on a better path now. The old path was like being in the woods without a compass—every turn led to being more lost. Now, her life was on a course of continual progress. The changes were indisputable. By applying focus, Ally was creating her own standards and living by her own rules. Ally was grateful for all the help she had from her mentor, Victoria. Everyone needs guidance once in a while, especially with financial issues. No one teaches you how to manage money. Parents do the best they can from what knowledge they've acquired, but sometimes they haven't acquired enough of the right knowledge and fly by the seat of their pants. You certainly don't learn it in school and it's tough to learn from others. Usually, money issues are hush-hush or people are offended at the mention of them. It's just too personal.

Because every household is unique, it's hard to emulate financial habits. The financial books in bookstores can be overwhelming. They cover everything and have so much information but it's too much to take in. All the technical financial information can be confusing and hard to digest—interest rates, FICO scores, taxes, IRAs, and investments. That's why Ally zoned out when she tried that route at the onset of her career. Someone once gave her a financial planning workbook as a gift—it was somewhere in the back of her closet, briefly perused but not read in entirety. She certainly didn't apply any of what she had read to her life.

If Ally had made one good decision in her life, it was that she sought help and it was so worth it. She felt a greater balance in her life and was optimistic about her financial security.

ONE YEAR AGO

Ally had been greeted at the door of the upscale boutique by a man in an impeccably tailored suit. The red carpet entry engulfed her in bright lights. She felt the bass thumping out exciting music and looked up at the monitor showing models wearing hot outfits. Glass cases were filled with sparkly accessories. It was intoxicating. And now she was standing in line, waiting to pay for her merchandise.

Ally was holding a bright blue top that she wanted to wear to a party that Saturday night. Having a new item to buy and thinking about how great she'd look in it gave her a rush. She was also holding a spangled black silk blouse, and a cute silver bracelet that matched both tops. She looked from left to right while waiting, making mental notes of other items that she wanted and would come back for.

Ally paid for her purchases and headed back to her office. The short walk was a welcome reprieve from her cubicle and she walked at an energetic pace. She was a young professional, her little shopping excursion was well-deserved, and she felt proud and accomplished. She was entitled to spend the money she made, right?

The weather had warmed after a cold winter and it felt as if everyone had spring fever. Ally stopped at a newsstand and picked up the latest issues of *Lucky* and *Cosmopolitan*.

When she was back at work, she focused on the workpaper file that needed attention. Before she was able to fully concentrate, she felt that deep, sinking feeling. That latent melancholy briefly surfaced from her solar plexus but she swallowed it back down, distracting herself with something on the Internet. Her credit card bill had come in the mail the previous week. She had made the minimum payment, but when she looked at the interest part of the balance, it was building. The money spent today was money she didn't have. She remembered thinking *Damn, it'll take me forever to pay that off. Oh, well.*

She put the bill in her junk drawer and tried not to think about it. It took some serious diversions to forget it. But living in a fantasy land was like living behind a façade. Her financial situation was filling her mind with worrisome thoughts lately and she couldn't ignore it any longer. For now, she was busy at work and would handle it another day.

After clearing a few things off her desk, she looked up at the clock. Three o'clock on Friday. She couldn't wait for the afternoon to go by. It was time to party.

"Hey, Taylor, we're still on for Happy Hour later, right?"

"Sure, I'll be there by six."

Their favorite Happy Hour locale was the typical Manhattan scene. It was a lively crowd of young, spirited professionals looking to get silly after work and maybe hook up for the evening. The young guys were good-looking movers and shakers.

Ally broached what was on her mind, hesitating a bit as she was not all that comfortable sharing her personal problems with friends. Taylor was a bit of an airhead anyway, and not the best listener when it came to serious issues. But Ally was feeling the post-shopping depression of knowing that she couldn't afford to indulge.

"I'm always broke and I feel like I'm working to constantly pay off a credit card bill," Ally told Taylor.

"You have the rest of your life to pay bills. Enjoy your life now! You'll only be young once. Besides, you want to look good, right?" Taylor laughed and flipped her hair over her right shoulder, eyes darting around looking for eligible men. Taylor was on a mission to find Mr. Wonderful. Her response was exactly what Ally expected. Taylor thought Mr. Wonderful would give her everything she wanted out of life.

"How come some people have it all? I want all the things I have plus security, not this constant money anxiety," Ally said as she watched Taylor give a come-get-me look to a dark-haired young man on the far side of the bar.

"You have a good job. What are you worried about?"

"I'm worried because I have no savings and a lot of debt," Ally said, trying to keep Taylor's attention.

"Come on, let's go over there." Taylor walked off, expecting Ally to follow as she made her way around the bar, closer to Mr. Prospect-of-the-Day.

Ally was tired of Taylor's short attention span. Taylor was a hot mess. She was deep in debt and with no direction, working at a dead-end job. She was so self-centered that once, when she wasn't attracting attention, she faked a fainting spell. Taylor had borrowed money from Ally more than once, and Ally had to chase her down to get it, which had almost ended their friendship. Ally thought, *I need new friends, not this narcissistic dingbat.*

Ally tolerated Taylor for another hour while Taylor trailed guys the entire time, making sure she looked available. After nine o'clock, the happy hour crowd thinned out and Ally told Taylor she needed to get home. By now, all the well-dressed guys that had arrived hours ago looked like sloppy drunken sailors, spitting and stumbling around.

The next day, Ally woke up and thought she had shaken that dour feeling, but the dark mood was with her all morning. She took the credit card bill out of the junk drawer and stared at it for a few minutes. That's all it took before she caved in to the sadness, and felt the depression coming on. *I can't afford to pay more than the minimum on this bill. And I have other things to pay for this month. I'm not getting ahead. Why do I keep spending money I don't have?*

Ally knew that she needed to find a better way. She wanted a good life with financial security. She wasn't even sure why she spent money the way she did. That little black spangled top she just bought? She had one just like it. She also didn't need the bright blue top. There was another blouse in her closet just as fancy—unworn, with the tags still on it.

She picked up the issue of *Cosmopolitan* she had bought yesterday. Cosmo is porn for twenty-something women. The first twenty pages were all fashion ads, meant to draw the viewer into their scenery. The models had that faraway look, like they were thinking the world revolved around them.

Maybe they were thinking that their world was so perfect and the world was lucky to have them in it. *Really?* It was more likely that they weren't thinking anything at all. Some of them looked as if they needed something to eat or were really stoned. Do the designers think anyone buys into these ads? *I guess so; otherwise, they wouldn't continue printing them.* Either way, it was all fantasy. None of what they were selling squared with reality. They were just too perfect. Ally had tried that shade of eye shadow and never looked that flawless. Apparently, lighting is everything.

Lucky was a shopping magazine. A spender's rag. There was always some new fashion advice and new product to tout. *What happened to last month's products? Old news, I guess. Or they make it seem that way, always playing on our insecurities, like we're just never good enough. But THIS product will be the answer to your problems. P-uuh-leez!*

Then Ally thought of the piled-up jars and the drawers stuffed with these products. After a few months, they lost their potency and needed to be replaced. Most didn't do what they promised. Ally couldn't remember what was in the drawers anymore. Some products were used once and then forgotten about. Hundreds of dollars … gone.

It seemed like these product ads just popped up out of nowhere. There were the constant emails and the images that danced across the monitor every time she was on her laptop. Marketing was more aggressive than ever. If you spent a dollar at any store, they started emailing every day. If you looked at their website, the items that were viewed would pop up on other webpages. There was no escaping the barrage of persuasion.

Apparently, she was one of the people who had bought into the flashy ads. Ally started questioning her behavior and it wasn't comforting. She looked over the credit card bill again. It was due in two weeks and the minimum interest charge was more than two hundred dollars. That was about all she could pay this month. As far as the regular balance, who knew when that would get paid?

The self-recrimination kicked in again. *I'm such a loser and I have nothing to show for my paycheck. Why am I buying things I don't need? Why can't I stop making foolish purchases? How come I can't get out of debt? How come I have no savings? How do I become financially secure?* Once in a while her logic switched on, but her denial over the past few months won out. Now, full reality set in and it was time to stop these self-destructive habits.

She thought of a friend of her mom's, Victoria. Victoria had it all. Wealthy, educated, confident—a picture of quiet success. It seems she did it on her own.

Ally wondered if she could learn from Victoria. She had never gained any knowledge from her own family and friends. Maybe it was time to entertain a new figure in her life and expand her circle of influence. She hoped that it wouldn't seem too imposing to ask someone to devote her time and wisdom to help her improve her situation.

Ally decided to have an informal discussion with Victoria, and called her mom to see if she could facilitate a meeting. After some small talk, she finally asked, "Do you still speak with Victoria?"

"Sometimes. Why do you ask?"

"Because I was hoping she could give me some financial advice. I'm getting further into debt and don't know what to do."

"I told you to stop the crazy spending. When you support yourself it's not so easy, is it? I'm sure it's fun to live in Manhattan and be around all the action, but it's expensive." Ally's mom thought for a second and added, "Let me call her and see if she would accept an invitation for a coffee chat."

Ally's mom called and the date was set.

MEETING HER MENTOR

Ally was still a toddler when her family moved to the suburbs. Victoria and her husband owned a local hardware store that served the young families that had moved from their city apartments to the new "country" developments. A house needed upkeep and Ally's parents visited the hardware store often. They always appreciated the help that Victoria and her husband provided; back then, customer service was personal.

Soon, Gail and Victoria were bumping into each other in town and stopping on the sidewalk to chat. Gail liked Victoria because she was open and friendly with everyone. Some of the other local business owners favored the residents that had high-paying jobs, and treated everyone else as commoners. Not Victoria. She enjoyed unscheduled sidewalk conversations, and no doubt it helped the business. They were prosperous.

Victoria and her husband blended into the community by participating in charity events. It was at those events that Gail and Victoria became good friends. They would sometimes spend Saturday afternoons together and occasionally, Victoria joined Ally's family for holidays and other celebrations. Victoria became a prominent figure in Ally's life, almost like a distant aunt.

Ally answered the door. Gail hadn't mentioned that Ally would join them, but Victoria was happy to see her.

"Hello, Allison honey!" Victoria's eyes sparkled. Petite in stature with smooth glowing skin, she was in her fifties but looked ten years younger. Ally admired Victoria's pale blue cashmere outfit, but it wasn't her clothes or her flawless complexion that made her so attractive.

She seemed elite, full of class and confidence. Ally was sure she had something to learn from Victoria. Victoria was a homeowner, a businesswoman, and a world traveler. She was comfortable in her own skin and managed to maneuver her way through life effortlessly. The opposite of Ally.

Ally was a little bit intimidated. She hadn't seen Victoria in years and it felt different now. She wasn't a silly little girl anymore. She wanted to live up to a higher standard and needed a role model. It felt like she was in the presence of royalty and Ally appreciated having such a person in her life. Victoria's energy was upbeat, just like the social queen that Ally remembered.

The ladies had coffee, tea, and cookies. They caught up on some lost time and then, finally, Ally told Victoria what was on her mind.

"Victoria, I really admire how you manage your life and feel I can learn from you. Would you mind letting me in on your secret? You seem to have it all."

Victoria looked surprised but delighted. She took a sip of her coffee. Her diamond pinky ring caught the sunlight coming in through the kitchen window and reflected shards of light on the wall.

"Why has this come up now?" Victoria asked..

"Well, I'm in a bit of debt and while I make decent money, it seems like I'm not getting ahead. I … I thought, from what I see of your life, that you could offer some suggestions." Ally's chin trembled slightly. She hoped it wasn't too noticeable.

"Of course," Victoria was quick to respond. Then added, "But I need to know that you'll follow my advice. I stopped sharing what I've learned with family and friends a long time ago because they dismissed it. I do want to help you but my time would be wasted if you were to ignore my suggestions."

Victoria waited for a response. She wanted to know that her recommendations would not fall on deaf, foolish ears. Ally would have to convince her that she was genuine and serious about her need for information. Victoria knew that people could be erratic; one day, they're into something, next day they're not. She also knew that sometimes young adults try to outdo each other, but have no idea what it takes to cover all the bases, in a financial sense. In some cases, she believed all they want is instant gratification. Or worse, that some have been so spoiled by their parents that they have no ability to learn adequate coping skills. She had encountered too many young people who only know how to put their hand out, and expect someone to bail them out when they're in over their heads.

Victoria prompted Ally for more information. "Why do you think I have the answers for you? What is it you're trying to achieve? Do you know what you want to achieve?"

Ally froze. She didn't have her thoughts together.

Victoria smiled at her. "Let's talk again next week. Bring some written goals so that we have a place to start. If you can show me that, I'll know that you're serious about this. You are welcome at my home next Saturday afternoon at two. I'll be waiting for you."

"Thank you, Victoria. I'm very serious about this and I'll be there."

VISIT ONE: DEFINING GOALS

Ally liked living on her own and she had been working for about five years now. Despite the fact that she was living with a roommate, she had her independence from her parents and embraced the memory of the day she moved out of her childhood home. Her degree in marketing gave her a decent corporate job. The hours were demanding but she had good benefits. Her employer offered a retirement plan, profit-sharing plan, and salary plus bonus. It was hard to reach the top bonus number that others were paid, but she worked as hard as she could. She liked working for a living, in spite of the workplace stress.

One thing Ally always appreciated about herself was being glad to see her name on a paycheck. Her attitude was unlike her friends who were relying on a man to give them a life. Her friends seemed to be on a path of College, Marriage, Leave Job to Have Kids. In the meantime, they didn't have a plan to take care of themselves. Ally was determined to be independent.

Ally knew that she was in the right place for opportunity. There was no better place to build her career. The wealth and money were right here. She saw it all around her—opulent skyscrapers, fancy restaurants, nicely dressed executives. If they had it, why couldn't she? It was time to combine optimism with thought and legwork. This wasn't going to happen just by dreaming about it. She knew she had to be smart. Like everything else, it required focused attention. She could do that.

Still, she had no money in the bank and was tempted by cool clothes and other things that her friends had. She was only making minimum payments on her credit card debt. At twenty-four percent interest, it would take her several years to pay off the entire balance. At this rate, the interest would start to accrue at a larger balance than the actual purchases. This wasn't the way to continue. It was definitely time to take steps in the right direction.

Ally would devote the time necessary to fulfill her need for knowledge about increasing her wealth. Everyone has time. In fact, everyone has the same amount of time. Time is free and available to be used as one wished. Time will transpire whether one spends it watching television, listening to the radio, or gaining an education. How each person spends her time determines the likelihood of the resulting benefits.

She refused to believe that the economy was to blame, that things were just too expensive, and that life only got harder. There were more millionaires than ever before and so many new ventures to invest in. In fact, this was the best time ever. Being educated and employed, Ally knew this had to be doable. It was a matter of managing things. Saving and investing were the keys; developing discipline to do both consistently was the challenge but certainly not an impossible one. And it was not just for certain people, it was for everyone.

Ally started to broaden her thoughts. From reading business magazines, she learned that as certain services and careers faded from existence, others were being created. Innovations were happening every day. New computer apps were being programmed, tested, and taken to the Web offering every convenience available on a handheld device. The Internet explosion was not slowing down; it was creating a new playing field. Life was constantly changing, and Ally wanted to ride the train. She was not going to work a dead-end job and made a commitment to her self-improvement. This was going to be step one of many steps to success.

Putting her thoughts together to determine goals was harder than she realized. She had to think about what she wanted. Did she want to own a Manhattan apartment? *Yeah, in my dreams. Everyone wants that.* It didn't hurt to dream big but her goals had to be simple and attainable for her to create a plan—such as having a healthy savings account and to be out of debt. To not live paycheck to paycheck. To be able to invest money. To feel a little freer, not like being constantly choked from a shortage of money. To feel she was getting ahead.

She definitely wanted a fulfilling career, and was on her way to getting that. She was at the beginning of her career path, but at least she had one. It seemed like a long road, but *no one starts at the top*, she told herself.

The following Saturday, Ally took the train to Victoria's town and walked from the train station to Victoria's house. She had her notebook and her questions with her. The beautiful spring day helped her feel a regeneration of spirit. This was a new beginning and the change of seasons matched her sense of renewal. She didn't know where to start and hoped she would gain that guidance from the first meeting.

Victoria lived in a quaint home in the corner of town, near Ally's suburban childhood home. Ally approached Victoria's home and took in the lovely landscaping. The house was not far from the sidewalk. A low white picket fence was set about halfway back on the front lawn. Behind the fence was an adorable two-tiered birdbath that attracted birds with a dribble of a gentle waterfall from the top level to the lower level. New buds were visible on the carefully clipped shrubbery and the annuals were poking up through the flower beds, waiting to flourish. A tiny garden fairy house was tucked under a shrub. It looked like a little dollhouse. That little area had the ambience of an enchanted garden. Small and nice, just like Victoria.

Victoria's house looked small from the outside. Inside, it was spacious yet cozy at the same time. The décor was fresh and updated. Every room had its own "personality." It was neat and clean with no clutter anywhere. Ally felt both welcomed and inspired as they sat down in Victoria's bright sunlit kitchen.

Ally took out her notebook and sheepishly opened to her list of goals. It was short. *How pathetic.* Her list only had 1) Save more, 2) Pay off credit cards, and 3) Invest. She mumbled something about not knowing know where to start. Victoria realized this and took the lead.

"I see that you have a designated notebook. That's a good sign. By the time we're done, I expect that notebook to be battered and worn. If it's as shiny and unmarked as it is now, then you won't have made the effort necessary to get what you want."

"Getting started with this was a lot harder than I thought," Ally admitted as her face twisted into a grimace.

"I know. Planning the action and navigating the changes requires organization of thought. But frustration is good because it causes you to take action. Healthy frustration leads to habit-changing behaviors. So be glad that you're frustrated. It means you're ready for a major change. Embrace the discontent you're feeling right now and use it to fuel your ideas and move away from your current situation," Victoria told Ally.

"I've never thought about frustration in that way." Ally's awareness was immediately enhanced. "I'm going to appreciate my negative feelings more often."

"Make sure that you examine your feelings carefully. You don't want to spiral yourself into constant self-doubt, but just enough to make you realize that you feel negativity for a reason. If it's something that needs to change, take comfort in the fact that you have what it takes to make changes in your life."

Ally exhaled slowly. No one had ever explained negative emotions to her that way before. Usually, other people were happy to see you dwell in your insecurities. Ally thought about all the times that she had let bad feelings drag her down and realized those were opportunities for change.

Victoria sensed the epiphany and felt it was time to backtrack a bit.

"Let me explain a few things about my beginnings. I didn't always have all this. I lived one step above a homeless person. I had shelter but it was far from comfortable. I lived in a dismal basement apartment. It was damp and rain leaked in from the window when the wind blew from a certain direction. It was uncomfortable all the time, cold in the winter and hot in the summer. And there were bugs. I learned to make the best of it. It was what I could afford."

Ally stared at Victoria in amazement.

"I was very focused on my career. I studied hard and became a CPA. At the time, I was in a corporate accounting department and, after a few years, was promoted to manager. I worked hard, saved all my bonus money and additional money from salary increases. It took many years, but I saved until I was finally able to put a small down payment on a two-bedroom foreclosure. I learned to dig my way out of that dismal basement room."

"So, all that was before you owned the hardware store?"

"Yes, I met my husband through a friend. His business was in its early stages when we first met. When the business expanded and we were married, I left my corporate job to run the store. He saw the potential in the new suburban developments and his vision paid off.

"Now, enough about me; back to you. Let's just talk in general about money for a little while," Victoria said. "For something that's really only a small piece of paper, it represents so many things in our lives. Did you ever look at it that way? Money's very closely tied to our basic needs. Our ability to have food, shelter, and clothing is all related to how we earn, spend, and use our money. For that reason, it's attached to our survival and is, therefore, emotionally loaded."

"Wow," Ally responded, fully tuned in. Ally had never really thought about money that way. To her and her friends, it was a means to be able to spend. She was now starting to see how narrow-minded her thinking was.

Victoria continued. "You need to realize that you're following deeply embedded behaviors right now. Everyone has them. It's not right or wrong, it just is. This is otherwise known as your money script. Money scripts are subconscious messages, often based on what you learned about money in your family when you were growing up. That's why they control behaviors that you are acting out. They can also be based on observations outside your family when growing up.

"Ultimately, you want to move toward or achieve the following healthy mindset wealth goals:

- Maintaining reasonable and low debt
- Having an active savings plan
- Having and following a conscious spending plan
- Enjoying a lack of conflict with family/partner around money
- Experiencing high levels of financial satisfaction
- Experiencing low levels of financial stress."

"Yes. That's the direction I want to move toward."

"Let's figure out a plan to get there. Work on your goals a bit; it will help you focus. But what I really want you to think about are the money messages that you've learned throughout your life. What is your most emotionally charged money situation that you can remember?"

Ally's shoulders dropped. "It was when I used to hear my parents talking quietly about the family's money issues. My mom would think I couldn't hear, but I knew that they were having tense financial discussions." Ally paused and looked up at the ceiling, remembering. "My mom tended to worry more than my dad did. At least that's how it seemed. The next day, they would act like nothing was wrong. They were very secretive and never taught me or my brother any financial lessons."

"That may be a reason for your head-in-the-sand attitude. Give yourself some time for self-reflection based on the messages you learned from your family. It will help you recognize what's transpiring now. Also, your goals right now are too broad and general. Expand each goal into a small plan. You want to save more? How much more? You want to pay off your credit cards? Have you given yourself a due date for that? You want to think about investing? What about goals for your career progress and saving for large purchases like a home? Take it in small steps but be specific."

Ally's head was spinning and she hoped she didn't look too confused taking all this in. She definitely felt that it was time well spent. It was eye-opening to relate early-life money messages to her current behavior. The list of goals seemed easier to work on. The soul-searching would take some thought but she was determined to give this a try.

The goal list had to include bringing her lunch to work. She spent way too much money on food during the work week. Sometimes it came to twenty or twenty-five dollars, after drinks and snacks. The morning gourmet coffee had to stop too, except for special occasions. At five dollars each, they add up. Maybe limit it to once a week. She estimated saving twenty dollars each day by bringing her lunch to work and skipping Starbucks.

With that thought in mind, she planned on transferring at least fifty dollars from her checking account to her savings account by the end of the week. She would figure out how to pay her bills and make it work.

VISIT TWO: STARING DOWN DEBT

Two weeks went by and Ally still had many unanswered questions about her finances. She was grateful that Victoria was agreeing to meet on a frequent basis.

"Hello Allison. How was your week?"

"I'm tired. I worked late three nights this week on a team project."

"But you're investing in your work experience. That's a great thing. Time invested in your career is never a waste."

"I know, but I hate working late. I feel like I have no time to myself."

"Unfortunately, that's what a career requires. Later on in your working years, you will have more choices open to you if you work hard now." Victoria stared hard to make the point sink in. Then she paused before asking, "So what have you done this week?"

Ally pulled out the notebook with her goals. "I'm looking up how to make healthy meals and take my lunch to work, and I went to the ATM a few days after I met with you. I transferred fifty dollars to my savings that day. When I went home, I figured out what my remaining bills were going to be. Then I planned how much of my next paycheck I would put away to build up my savings. I'm going to do that every two weeks after I get paid."

"That's excellent." Victoria gave a thumbs-up. "You've taken immediate action. You have no idea what a milestone that is. Mentally, that breaks your current pattern. Some people never get there. Now, your job is to make it a habit—a lifelong habit."

Victoria cut up tea sandwiches and set them on small plates, placing one in front of Ally. She was pleased that she had made an impact on someone's financial well-being.

"This is great. We're off to a good start and I want to keep the momentum going. Let's continue talking about money scripts. Have you thought about other messages you may have received over the years?"

"Yes, I was always jealous of a childhood friend who was given everything she wanted. She purposely put things in my face if it was something new. I had a few nice things, but certainly not as much as she had."

"Those memories provoke powerful feelings, don't they? And to associate those emotions with that scenario can be so profound, you may not even realize how those feelings have been embedded in your brain and are now responsible for your current overspending."

Ally leaned in. This was such a revelation.

"These hard-to-break money scripts are attached to emotional or traumatic money experiences. The logic that you rationalized from the experience with your childhood friend may have helped you deal with uncomfortable feelings in that situation. But while your script has served you by being partially true, you need to recognize that it is also partially false.

Your friend manipulated your feelings to feel superior to you. You don't know how all her possessions were obtained. Her parents may well have overextended themselves to provide all that. Therefore, you were left with only a negative sense of longing that you didn't have what she did, and she used it to make you feel bad about yourself. Are you seeing where this is going?"

"Yes, I do now. I realized many years later that she wasn't a very good friend, but for other reasons."

"It will help you to identify your money scripts. Narratives are imprinted within our brains and the stories keep replaying in an endless loop, directing our energy toward poor decisions that seem logical. In spite of having control over our adult lives, the old scripts manage our decisions, however detrimental. If these harmful scripts are not addressed, they never change."

"You're so right. When I buy something, I think about who I will impress. And yet, I know I can't afford it. I'm also giving in to my old feelings of inferiority, which evolved from interacting with an insensitive, selfish person. I had such low self-esteem when I was growing up, and others fed off that. I can also remember being surrounded by so many children of wealthy families. They were dressed really nicely and had the most expensive clothes and bags. They all had an abundance of expensive jewelry. We weren't like that and I think I'm overcompensating for it now. I wish I had known better back then but I never had much of a support system at that age. I always felt very isolated and misunderstood."

"Everyone operates from money scripts, so you're not alone. Acknowledging and examining the old money scripts is critical to moving toward the necessary changes to escape the powerful hold of the old messages."

Ally shifted uncomfortably and felt a spike of difficulty. She was starting to recognize innate patterns where she wasn't sure why she did things the way she did. She reacted to certain situations in ways she regretted afterward. The unpleasant memories felt like chains. "Is there a way to get past this? I don't want to keep sabotaging myself because of experiences I had when I was twelve years old."

"It starts with the identification of the behaviors. Identifying, examining, and acknowledging the behaviors allow an opportunity to recognize when they surface. When you invoke your conscious, rational thought, it gives you time to change your decision. Take your time with this aspect of the process. It will help to keep a journal. Use your notebook not only for your goals but to fully explore your past thought patterns. While you're writing, don't judge your feelings, acknowledge them," Victoria explained.

"This is going to take some time," Ally replied.

"That's OK, just do it and you'll feel the difference." Victoria asked to see Ally's goals again. She was glad to see that Ally was using her notebook since writing down goals is one way of ensuring that you have intentions of achieving them.

Ally's goal list was short but it was better than last week's abbreviated phrases:

1. Transfer fifty dollars to savings every payday
2. Bring (healthy) lunch to work every day

3. Pay off credit cards

4. Fund employer retirement accounts

"Appreciate yourself for starting," Victoria said. "If you make up your mind to develop good money habits, it will become easier. Take small steps for now while we begin to unwind and understand the process behind your actions."

"I put fifty dollars into my savings and started taking lunch to work, but it doesn't feel like that will get me to where I want to be."

"Give yourself some credit. We'll work through this and you can use me as a sounding board," Victoria reassured Ally.

"Now, let's address the personal debt. You realize that you need to pay it off as quickly as possible, right? We need to create a plan to pay off your debt. How much debt do you have right now, Allison? If you are paying interest, you are throwing money away. Debt will burden you and it won't go away if you pretend it's not there."

Ally was embarrassed to say how much she owed on her credit cards. It was more than eight thousand dollars. At twenty-four percent interest, the interest portion of the payment was more than one hundred fifty dollars. She only paid about two hundred dollars each month and tended to add purchases. It wasn't moving in her favor. She would be in debt for a very long time if she didn't do something soon.

When Ally finally admitted how much she owed, Victoria frowned. She paused for a few seconds to think of how to change things.

"How much rent do you pay for your Manhattan apartment?" Victoria asked.

"Eighteen hundred a month and I have a roommate." As the words were leaving her mouth, Ally knew she couldn't afford to live in Manhattan anymore.

"You need to move. You're paying too much in rent. You will never be able to pay your bills and save any money if you continue on this path," Victoria told Ally. "Your next step is to look for a more affordable place to live. It may cost you some time in commuting, but you can use your time on the train for reading. With the money you'll save in rent, you'll pay off your credit card debt. Understand?"

Victoria was crystal clear and she was right. Ally should have done this long ago. It was crazy to think that her paycheck would increase faster than her debts would pile up. If she could save even five hundred a month in rent, even if she had to buy a train ticket to get to work, it would help to pay down the credit card balance.

"You'll start the plan to pay down your credit card debt and match it with a savings plan. You may have to suspend your buying habits for a while but in the long run, you'll feel much better about your situation."

"You're right. I think I can move out of Manhattan to where the rent is much more affordable," Ally admitted. "I can probably save five hundred to seven hundred fifty dollars a month."

Ally left that day with a new perspective. It was time to get real and deal with her credit card debt, not sweep the problem under the proverbial carpet.

Goal number five was to look for a more affordable apartment. Her next step would be to move as quickly as possible, even if it meant subletting.

The next day, Ally did an online search for studio apartments in Brooklyn and

Queens. She decided to make at least three phone calls for the first two days and schedule two appointments before the end of the week.

SMOKE AND MIRRORS

Ally rode the train to get to the library in Victoria's neighboring town to attend one of the presentations Victoria frequently made at local libraries. Victoria felt she needed to help people who might not have had anyone to learn from, and the feedback was rewarding. She approached the podium without notes but with her quiet confidence intact.

Doesn't it seem as if some people have everything? They have the latest designer goods, drive flashy cars, and take extravagant vacations. It seems like the good times will never end. Well, it might surprise you to know that most people are living far beyond their means. What they have, they have today. Their outer appearance must be supported by large sums of money. In reality, their situation is precarious at best. If the money river were to slow to a trickle, their standard of living would drop dramatically.

One of my first life lessons was from childhood neighbors. My family moved to a brand-new home in a just-built development when I was ten years old. The family next door had a daughter, Felicity, who was nine. Our families became friends and Felicity and I became pals. Their home was the larger of the two models built in the development, decorated with the finest furnishings. They lived a very comfortable life. The mom didn't work and dad was president of a profitable family-owned business. All three children had the best of everything to excess. Mom stayed within the traditional boundaries of a good wife. She cooked and cleaned all week and then spent all day Saturday in the beauty parlor getting her hair dyed and prettified. Mom drove the latest El Dorado. A Cadillac was the popular car back then; it was a status symbol for wealth. Hers was a special edition, a metal-flake crimson-colored custom machine. It was more than a car, it was dressing for the driveway—and it matched the color of mom's hair.

The entire family had an air of snootiness, as if they were better than everyone else. They lived their perfect life in their suburban bubble and no one else's life compared to their perfect lifestyle. To be sure, you only needed to ask them.

Within two short years, they needed to move into a small apartment, leaving the big suburban home behind. No more central vacuum, central air-conditioning, waterfront backyard. No more interior decorators and custom furniture. I wonder if the white baby-grand piano fit in their apartment.

I must admit, at my young age, two years seemed like a long time. But to an adult, two years is a blip on the radar.

What happened? Well, the business, run by dad and his brothers, began to fail because they weren't getting along quite as well anymore. Dad left the business and went ahead with a painting business. That didn't work out, so they invested their savings in a small luncheonette. Luncheonettes used to be places where the neighborhood residents would gather to enjoy an egg cream or ice-cream cone. But that was in the 1950s and 1960s. Fast-forward to the 70s—these busi-

nesses were not the popular hangouts that they once were. That business did not pan out the way they thought it would.

Very shortly thereafter, life took a drastic turn. The shock was too much and it affected mom's health. Well into her forties and not able to deal with her life being downsized, she began to have panic attacks. Those panic attacks were justified. She only knew how to clean her house and go to the beauty parlor. She never learned any skills and never held a job. When times were good, she fell into complacency as they watched their standard of living rise. But when the tide went out, they were left naked and mom got a dose of reality. She had no means of income and no work experience. Therefore, she had no currency to add to their standard of living.

Within ten years, dad died of a heart attack. We lost touch with that family but it taught me a lesson that I'll never forget.

Don't get ahead of yourself in life. Don't think you're something you're not, because life has a way of giving you a reality check. The good times may not last forever.

People look like they have it all, when most times they don't. It's all smoke and mirrors. Being comfortable and pretending to be wealthy are two different things. When money is constantly coming in, it masks underlying secrets. If the constant flow of money isn't there, whether it's to pay the minimum credit card bill or allow for constant spending, the consequences can be devastating. It leaves an exposure that may be so difficult to overcome that it may take years to recover.

Don't be fooled by people who look like they have it all or are boastful of what they have. They may have their material possessions but they also have the bills. It amazes me how people lie to themselves about their debt. They think it will magically go away on its own or that they have forever to pay it off. As long as they have "things" now, they're happy.

A home's exterior is a shell of normalcy that encases a scrambled mix of complex relationships. Each family conducts its affairs in its own unique way. The shell also encases a variety of dysfunction.

People who have "things" wind up needing to go to work every day to pay for all those "things." There was a popular bumper sticker years ago that read, "I owe, I owe, so off to work I go." People want immediate gratification so they buy everything that they want all at once. A new car or SUV, new furniture, clothes, CDs, sound systems. Then when the bills need to be paid—and they're coming—they are on the spending treadmill. Life requires certain payments every single month, like mortgage or rent, food, utilities, etc. Now add the bills for all the "things." Then throw some unexpected expenses in, like birthday presents, medical emergencies, car repairs, repairs for a broken appliance, weddings, and soon the payments are chasing them. It becomes an endless cycle of constant spending, constant bill paying, followed by more spending and more bills. If they hadn't started with a mountain of debt, a little planning could have mitigated the constant payment urgencies. It only takes one month for the bill paying to become difficult.

If the running theme of your life is to constantly acquire material things, you need to change your perspective.

It was great seeing you today. I hope this afternoon has been beneficial for you.

MONEY MINDSETS

For Ally's next visit, Victoria planned a trip to the mall. It was one of the biggest, fanciest malls in the country. As they walked through, passing the decorated windows that displayed the coolest clothes, shoes, accessories, and every last trinket you could imagine, Victoria watched for Ally's reaction.

Ally almost tripped over her feet a few times, drawn to store windows, making U-turns as merchandise caught her eye. Marketing is so sophisticated now that it's almost impossible not to be drawn into the stores to spend, spend, and overspend. The marketers actually make you feel like you can't live without their merchandise. They constantly advertise sales, as if "Spend more, save, more!" is actually true.

Victoria laughed to herself thinking about how many people are sucked into those marketing ploys. *How can you be saving if they're continuing to take more money from you?*

When they were near the food court, Victoria suggested that they sit and have a drink. This was going to start her lesson for the afternoon.

"Allison, I noticed that you were drawn to many stores here as we took our short walk."

"It's hard not to spend with temptation in every window. It starts to trigger my personal high," Ally admitted.

"There are several different things going on here that I want you to keep in the back of your mind. First, you're working off your money script. The belief that you were deprived and need to have the best new items to feel good about yourself is alive and well but not serving your current well-being. Second, the salespeople of the world have figured out how to get you to give them the money that you have earned. Advertising, fantasies, quick availability, and instant gratification—they all trigger pleasure sensors. If it were up to the advertisers and merchandisers, you would spend all your money on their products. They have no regard for your financial well-being, your security, your need for shelter, food, and clothing. They have basically redefined what society now considers 'needs.' Several decades ago, most families never dreamed of owning fancy cars, taking lavish vacations, and decking out their homes. Life was simpler and no one knew differently. 'Wants' and 'needs' are almost synonymous now.

"The ease of credit is another way that merchandisers are emptying your pockets. Several decades ago, most households did not have credit accounts. It was the exception, not the norm. Now, the norm is for everyone to have multiple credit cards—at high interest rates. That's how they manage to keep you providing them with a constant cash flow.

"The rational mind is not as strong as the impulsive mental functions. If you add stress, indecision, or confusion to the setting, the cognitive rational brain functions will be interrupted and lead to poor financial management. Emotional responses interfere with decision making. You see this when people go on shopping sprees when they've had a bad week or a fight with a spouse."

Ally recalled how she had allowed these outside influences to bait her actions. "How do I change this?" she asked.

"Remember the healthy wealth achievements? In addition to a savings plan, you need a spending plan. We are 'wanting machines' and will spend endlessly. The spending plan will be in conjunction with some behavioral changes to avoid acting on impulse. A good remedy is to create some space between your impulse to buy and the actual buying behavior."

"Can you give me some suggestions?"

Victoria spoke with emphasis. "Reflect on your feelings and take some time away from your temptations before giving in to them. It will help to find ways to enjoy life without spending beyond your budget. Find an affordable activity and plan your day so that you don't have idle time to be distracted by marketers. If you do feel like spending, plan on having a list of inexpensive things to buy such as a book or a magazine. Go to the library, go for a walk, go to the pond to feed the ducks, watch TV, bake a cake, or watch a movie at home instead of going to the movies. Trick your mind into finding pleasure in things that aren't costly. When you can spend one weekend without spending money, you'll feel so much better. At the end of the month, you'll realize that you were able to save."

"OK, I get it," Ally replied, knowing that this is where the rubber would meet the road. *Not give in to my impulsive spending? Uh-oh.*

"Everyone is trying to take your money; you can't even look at email without being enticed. Don't buy into the ads, and avoid the traps. Think of yourself first," Victoria implored. "Once that money is spent, you won't get it back."

Victoria continued, hoping to flood Ally with ideas, "Carry as little cash as possible. Cash has a way of disappearing when it is readily available."

"I never thought that was necessary … I've always worked," Allison responded.

"Yes, you have always worked, but your hard-earned money is going straight to retailers. You're not making accommodations for yourself. You need to take a vacation from spending and see what that feels like. The money that you don't spend will start your consistent habit of paying yourself first. Save first and live off the rest.

"As far as planning your spending—"

"A spending plan? Please explain."

"As I was saying, if you are serious about your financial security, you need to shop in outlet stores only, at least for now. Buy merchandise off-season, when things are on sale, not when the goods first hit the stores. Wait until August or September to buy summer clothes; wait until January and February to buy winter clothes. Don't buy anything until you can save up first. And don't forget unexpected purchases. That's why you'll first want to put away six- to eight-months' spending money. Even though you're only starting with fifty to one hundred dollars each month, you'll have saved something."

Victoria waited until Ally stopped scribbling in her notebook. When it looked like Ally was ready to take in new information, she moved on to some more ideas.

"Here's a few other suggestions. Learn to refurbish and update old things, and buy accessories such as scarves, jewelry, or a different jacket that matches several pieces of your existing wardrobe."

Ha! Ally rarely thought of that. She had so many mismatched pieces and continued buying when something lacked a compatible item.

"Let me tell you how easy it is to get sucked into a debt situation. As all my college friends started working, we became accustomed to having money. My close friend went and bought himself a nice, sporty car. As if that wasn't unnecessary enough, the following year he upgraded to the newest model of the same car. The salesman told him to buy now because next year's prices were going to be much higher! He fell for that sales pitch and wound up being thirty thousand dollars in debt one year out of school. Then, when his prospects at his job couldn't seem worse, he injured himself and had to go on disability.

"Don't ever buy into a salesman telling you to buy now because prices will go up. I have heard that time and time again. You know what? Sometimes, next year's prices aren't higher. If they do increase, it may not be by much. Business models dictate that the sooner they have your money, the better off they are. If you take some time to decide on a purchase, you may find that you didn't really need it and will have kept your money.

"Marketing has become so sophisticated and research now starts with infancy. They are hoping to create lifetime customers. You can always wait for a promotional deal. When the retailers figure out that you won't pay full price, they'll drop the price to get something out of you. Wait for a sale; you don't need to be the first to own everything."

Ally sat back and let this all sink in. "It's time for me to go home."

"I see that." Victoria sensed that she might have broken through the wall of a cemented lifestyle pattern.

Ally's plan for this week's lesson was to go home and look through everything she owned. All of her old clothes, books, shoes, and other stuff. What she couldn't wear anymore would get donated. Instead of being frustrated with what she had with a constant need for more, she would re-create what she already owned for a new look. She chose three old sweaters and decided to find a jacket in her closet to match all three. Until then, she would not buy anything new.

Victoria had recommended buying accessories that could be worn with many outfits. New, inexpensive jewelry would make an old outfit look new. Ally would be sure to make better decisions and never buy anything unless it had multiple uses.

Ally was going to look at studio apartments tomorrow, and was getting ready to move even though she hadn't signed a lease yet. She had been thinking about buying a few new things to replace her old furniture. Thinking on a different wavelength now, she stared at her old bedside table. Based on what Victoria had told her, she instead decided to repaint it. That would make it unique. She decided on a deep tangerine and realized that she would never be able to create an accent look of that nature if she bought a brand-new table. Not only could the table be painted, but she could update colors all over with a little bit of paint or fabric. Then, if she wanted any new décor items, they would have to be secondhand from a garage sale or bought at a deep discount.

ONE MONTH'S PROGRESS

Ally's mind was filled with all the new information she had learned over the past few weeks. It was new, exciting, and frightening at the same time. There was still so much to learn. For now, she was taking the first major step by deciding to move. It was encouraging to know that Victoria was fully engaged in her progress. While Ally wanted to see and feel quicker results, she settled into working the plan.

Victoria began by asking, "What have you learned this month?"

"I'm still working on moving from my current apartment to a studio. The rent on a studio will save me money and I've already looked at several in Brooklyn and Queens. They're near the trains, so I'll have a fairly easy commute. I must have been crazy to think I could live in Manhattan. All that rent is killing me. There are a couple of possibilities in Queens—in Forest Hills or Bayside. I revised my goals to include paying off the credit cards with the money saved from a lower rent. I also have a list of questions."

"Sounds good. Let's take a look."

Updated goals from previous visit:

1. Transfer fifty dollars or more to savings every payday

2. Bring (healthy) lunch to work every day

3. Pay off credit cards four hundred dollars per month (with money saved from rent)

4. Fund employer retirement accounts

5. Look for a more affordable (studio) apartment

"I still have some confusion over whether I should save money or pay my credit card debt."

"Pay off the credit cards first. You'll incur additional costs in interest if you keep those balances high. Pay off the credit card with the highest interest rate. Make the minimum payments on the remaining accounts. Continue doing that until you pay them all off. One other thing. Cut up all but one credit card. Don't close the accounts; just stop using the lines of credit. If your credit limits are increased, call and say you don't want them increased. Those lines of credit are looked at if you apply for a mortgage or other loan. The lenders assume that you will use the entire amount of your credit lines and be overextended. You don't want to have inflated lines of credit that you don't need.

"Remember," Victoria warned, "you'll have to suspend the use of credit for a while. Pay for things in cash and then you won't have to worry about adding to your high balances."

"I have another question. How do I build up an emergency fund?"

"Keep consistent with your current savings plan. Have a goal in mind. At fifty dollars a month, you will have six hundred dollars saved in one year. If you can do more, great.

Reassess your plan throughout. Stay focused on your goal and you'll have the amount that you aim for."

Ally nodded in agreement. She had saved that fifty dollars and realized that she didn't miss it. Now, onto the next question.

"Is it OK to spend? Ever?"

"Great question. Yes it is, in accordance with your spending plan. You need both a savings plan and a spending plan. If you incur costs that increase your working skills or help you apply for a higher-paying job, that would be money well spent. If you buy books that educate you, that would be money well spent. You need to make some initial corrections in your habits and save some money first before making any unnecessary purchases, but always remember to invest in yourself first."

"OK, got it." Ally understood Victoria's reasoning and agreed with the plan. But Victoria wasn't finished.

"Let's talk about spending. Plan spending and save for purchases in advance. Make a list of things that you need. Buy them one at a time, not all at once running up a huge credit card balance. Pay each item off one at a time, while saving for bigger expenses. Alternate months when spending for big items and focus on one need at a time. Note the word *need.*

"If this is the year that you devote to paying off your credit card debt, focus on that goal for now. Maybe that takes three years. I paid off my house over a four-year period while saving fifty thousand dollars at the same time."

"That's amazing, Victoria! How did you do that?"

"I was disappointed that I only had three thousand dollars to my name. I was able to pay my bills and support my lifestyle but I was frustrated with my job and felt stressed out all the time. I had an irrational manager and, after a notable disagreement, I decided that I was not going to be a corporate slave. While I always liked working, I didn't want to be trapped into having to keep a job that I didn't like. I wanted to run my life, not have my life run me. It was a daunting goal, I have to admit. But I knew that if I did the right thing, I would feel much better. I started by beefing up my savings while making double payments on my home mortgage."

"How quick was your progress?"

"I started by building on my three thousand dollars and after one year, I had sixteen thousand dollars saved. I had split my bonus money toward the savings goal and the mortgage paydown."

"That's amazing." Ally could not even imagine taking on a plan of that magnitude. *According to Victoria's story, it can be done. I guess the same could apply to paying off student loans.* "I have friends who are buried under their debt and feel like they'll never pay it off."

"They will. You can pay off your debt too if you bite the bullet now, while you're in the prime of your career. It will benefit you in your later years. If you have a stressful job now where you work long hours, you may be able to trade that in for a less stressful, lower-paying job fifteen or twenty years from now."

"What's a good way to feel more secure now?"

"Make sure to stay ahead of your rent payment by at least three paychecks. Right now, you should divide your income into rent, credit card paydowns, and savings. As you increase your income, you'll be able to allocate your money toward more goals."

Ally decided on a method to focus her plans. After spending some time alone, reflecting, she realized that she had to come up with a weekly system to move forward. This focus infused energy into her intentions. She decided that each Monday she would come up with three mini-goals for the week. Whether it meant saving money on lunch, bargain-shopping for a specific item, or walking a different way to avoid a certain store, she would start each week with three small, attainable targets. Each following day of the week, she identified two or three small actions with the mini-goals in mind. These little actions would help accomplish the weekly goal. By having a small win each day, the momentum started to build. After two or three days, the progress felt rewarding.

By the end of the week, her small actions became habits. She reflected on what she had learned. How hard or easy was it to do without impulse purchases? Did she feel uncomfortable not giving into temptations? How much money did she save by not spending each day? What times of the day are the worst? Did it make her depressed to know that she was limiting her spending? How strong was the sense of accomplishment from sticking with her goals?

Ally noted the times and days that she was ready to give in. It was usually right after payday. She made a note to add something to her program. She would need a psychological diversion to offset her periods of weakness.

Ally sat down and wrote a spending plan. She made a list of the purchases that she delayed and planned on when she would buy them. The earliest would be three months from now. Each item would be bought one at a time, even if it was needed before then. She would have to do without until the following month.

Ally made up her mind to be optimistic about the process, not think of it as if her life were coming to an end. There would be plenty of shoes, clothes, and jewelry to buy when her bills were paid off. She would make the best of what she had now, and she had plenty. Besides, this was starting to get interesting. While she learned to cook, she found a neat by-product. Who needed to pay for an expensive facial when you could steam vegetables and your face at the same time by standing over the pot? Halfway through, when poking a fork through the vegetables, she could cover them back up and then make a run for the exfoliant. *Who says you can't be creative?*

FINANCIAL MINDSET

Victoria's next speech topic was one that Ally was interested in hearing more about. She settled in with the other ladies in the library's basement meeting room.

Let's talk about your financial mindset and how it's responsible for your decisions.

What does money represent to us? Safety, freedom, respect, reward, power, an identity. It's also a ticket to dreams, and a symbol for love, hope, and promises.

It allows us to be able to take care of our children.

It's a cause for worry, stress, and depression.

It creates social barriers of inclusion and exclusion.

Money brings us together or separates us.

It can be a force of manipulation or a motive for murder.

How about being an aphrodisiac? It's how women size up men sometimes, isn't it? We don't always want to admit it, but the old tribal tradition of marrying a daughter off to a man of means still has value, doesn't it?

Sometimes it's a cause for resentment, if someone becomes forced into having to take over financial responsibilities.

The emotional attachments to money are endless. I want to take this time to explore how prevalent a part money plays in society.

For women, sometimes their choice of a spouse determines their social and financial security. Women may find it easy to disconnect from money issues because, in society, it's not tied to their identity. Women tend to use beauty as a currency in exchange for their ability to have wealth. Other attributes that women exchange for wealth are health, fertility, nurturance, and ability to be the main caretaker. Women are conditioned to believe that they should convert their domestic skills into financial security or they risk losing their feminine appeal.

This trade-off results in a swap of virtues and beliefs for economic security. Think about how this permeates the foundation of our lives, of how we're supposed to live our lives. Female-based roles going to back to Leave It to Beaver portray and validate those beliefs.

Daughters who were never taught about money are severely underserved. All these theories cause inequality in the workplace to persist and social inequalities such as unequal pay based on gender.

In this way, women are perceived to be dependent, needy, and vulnerable. Even when women take charge of their lives with a career and become an equal family breadwinner, there is a strong contradiction in the family roles—working mom or stay-at-home mom? Women even work against each other. Working moms criticize stay-at-home moms and stay-at-home moms criticize working moms. No one wins.

What a contrast to how money and men are perceived. For men, their manhood and identity are attached to their financial aptitude. Men buy expensive gifts to prove their worth; women use money to bond and create relationships. While men use money to show power, women will downplay finan-

cial differences to enhance connections. In their quest for money, it is not unusual for men to put their finances first and family second.

These social perceptions put too many expectations on men and not enough on women. Men are expected to bear the financial burdens and make the financial decisions. Women are taught not to be concerned with their financial status.

But what happens when that doesn't work according to plan? It would be very convenient to know, as a young woman, that someone will take care of you. That would offer a guaranteed life promise. But, when men abandon their end of the deal, women are left with a lack of alternatives or worse, with nothing. By not setting up the alternatives early on, before the tidal wave of divorce, medical problems, abandonment, or the demands of a large family comes crashing down, women are left with the fear of finding themselves homeless and alone. Many are in fear of going broke or not having enough money to retire.

Women's financial independence should be a central element to their sense of identity, not an accident.

I encourage all of you to challenge your learned perceptions. If it's a freeing perception, then go with it. Find ways to expand on your perception. If it's a limiting perception, then find the alternative.

After a moment of silence, the small group of women stood up and applauded in admiration.

REPLACING FINANCIAL RELATIONSHIPS

Ally and Taylor met for lunch one month after Ally's initial visit with Victoria. Taylor started a nonstop ramble about some hot guy she saw in a bar. "I went up to him and asked him for a cigarette."

"But you don't smoke," Ally reminded Taylor.

"I know, but he was cute and it was all I could think of," Taylor replied as she checked texts on her phone.

Ally noted that Taylor had an expensive leather phone holder. "Nice phone cover. Where did you get it?"

"At Brighton. Isn't it cute? It has little travel images on it. I'll be going all those places someday."

"Sure you will," Ally agreed, trying not to be a downer, but laughing on the inside.

"So Ally, where have you been? What have you been doing?"

"I've been visiting with a friend of my mom's for financial advice and—"

"Sounds boring."

Taylor had the attention span of an ant. Her eyes flitted back and forth, looking for excitement. She could barely listen to anything, unless it was about her.

Taylor challenged Ally. "So, what does she tell you?"

Ally wasn't sure Taylor was interested so she made it brief, not expecting Taylor to ask for details.

"She tells me all kinds of things about being self-sufficient, building wealth, securing my future, and saving for emergencies. Did you ever think about how your financial mindset determines your money?"

"No. What do you mean by that?"

Before Ally had a chance to respond, Taylor went on.

"Who cares? Don't you want to live a great lifestyle now?" Taylor blurted out. She dismissed any form of discipline.

"I would love to live a great lifestyle now but I also want to have a great lifestyle in general. That means I'm taking actions now to prepare for emergencies and for the future. I have no money saved. Do you?"

Taylor rolled her eyes. She was too self-absorbed to focus on delayed gratification skills. "Yeah, I have a 401(k) at work that I put some money into." Then, she began babbling about a party their friend Jennifer was having.

Ally realized she was on a different wavelength than Taylor. Maybe it was a result of Taylor's having been spoiled her whole life. Everything had been handed to her. Her parents paid her entire college tuition and then bought her a brand-new sports car when she graduated. Now that she was on her own, she didn't know how to make decisions on her own. She had never had any good role models. Her parents were spendthrifts too.

"Well, I don't know if I can make it to the party but I'll let you know. I need to get back to work. It was good seeing you."

"OK, call me soon."

Ally was glad lunch was over. It was too bad that she and Taylor were moving in different directions. Ally had met Taylor when they started college and they remained friends after graduation. They both worked in the city and both had good entry-level career skills. But it seemed in the last few months that the friendship, based on the common ground of education, was fading fast. Ally was ready to move on and if she wanted to change the direction of her life, she would have to distance herself from Taylor. It just didn't make sense to stay friends with someone who had the potential to sabotage her efforts. Ally needed to align herself with like-minded people who would be supportive.

Ally knew what she wanted and was glad she was taking steps toward her goals, even if she was starting slowly. She didn't want to rely on anyone, especially a guy. Ally wanted her own house, her own safety net, and she wanted to build her own wealth. Ally wanted the gratification of knowing that she could do it on her own and make her own choices.

If you don't make your own life decisions, someone else will make decisions for you. She remembered reading that saying somewhere and it scared her. After a childhood of listening to everyone telling her what to do, she didn't want to have her adult life dictated to her. She remembered her mother constantly telling her what she could or couldn't have. And at Christmas, when she hoped she would get what she asked for, she was always disappointed with some less expensive version of it. Her mother was good at making sure she didn't have high expectations. It seemed like the constant deprivation only created more of a want for things. In Ally's case, it was not only a want for things, but a want *to develop the ability to have them*. That would be the version of success that she would want for herself.

Remembering the limitations that her mother placed on her, she realized that early patterns learned from parents are so deeply engraved that they're almost impossible to shake. Her mother never went to college but insisted that Ally get a degree. That was a positive, but then there were the many negatives. Her mother made her feel that she couldn't be original and creative, and that the good things in life were out of reach so she should settle for whatever was offered, and not ask for more. At least Ally was different—she learned to reject these limiting thoughts. Some people stay chained by these influences their whole lives. She didn't go to college to settle for mediocrity.

At the same time, Ally knew that the differences between her and her friends were the things they learned from their parents, especially how their mothers had influenced their habits. Taylor's mom spent money like crazy and doled out money to Taylor if she needed it. She robbed Taylor of developing her own coping skills and prolonged her immaturity.

Some moms influenced their daughters' decisions to get married so their daughters would be taken care of. That's why many of Ally's friends were on a mission to find a man and spent their entire paychecks thinking that they would have someone to take care of them. Some women think that if a man isn't there for them, they can fall back on their parents. But what will happen when their parents are gone? Do they expect to be taken care of by their siblings? That's an indulgent imposition—one not likely to happen. Plus, it breeds tension and resentment.

Taylor's money script was that the money would never end. She was using her feminine charm in exchange for economic security and responsibility. There you go, just like Victoria said.

Those money scripts would have to be tamed or it would lead to disaster. If things went according to plan, Taylor would have the fairy tale she dreamed of. If not, well … there were too many negatives to consider.

Ally was starting to recognize her own money scripts and acknowledge her thoughts. She would not give in to immature behavior and risk turning her life over to someone else. The limiting thoughts her mother had taught her would be disposed of and replaced by purposeful actions. It was a bit challenging to reflect on all these thoughts. Most of them were attached to negatively charged emotional experiences and moments of ugly awareness. But it was necessary to acknowledge them and allow the old feelings to come back.

Ally did her best to acknowledge these feelings without judgment, and after trying a few times it became easier. She practiced when she was walking from her job to the train at the end of the work day. She let the memories come back and thought about her mother's influence. Why did her mother set her up to be limited in thought and creativity? It was an exercise in awareness to realize that parents probably had some reason based on what they were taught or some irrational fear. Either way, the old thoughts didn't make sense now. It was time to throw them away. Sort of like a mental cleaning. The cobwebs in her brain were still wrapped around those old suggestions and it was time to sweep them out. What was just as critical, though, was replacing the old thoughts with new, enriching thoughts.

Despite her apprehensions, she was sure this could be done while living well. There was no reason to live a life of deprivation as long as she was taking steps toward her goals.

She already had taken a big step by moving to a studio in Queens. It was small and partially underground, but she didn't need a roommate and was more comfortable living by herself.

MENTAL BREAKTHROUGH

At their next meeting, Ally was ready with her questions.

"Victoria … so now that I've moved to a studio apartment, I started to make a budget but I'm not sure I have it right."

"Let's start with a clean notebook page. Begin with your income. Add up all of your income. Acknowledge that it's all you have to work with.

"Now, let's start listing your expenses. Under the caption of expenses, I want you to put your name as the first item. Then start listing your obligatory expenses. Don't cheat and leave out expenses like haircuts. They are obligatory expenses, just like your rent and utilities. I know that rent and utilities are expensive. I think your choice to move out of an expensive apartment into a less costly place is great. If your minimum living expenses are high now, you have to focus on increasing your income and containing your obligatory expenses. How much of your monthly net income goes toward your minimum living expenses?"

"About fifty percent."

"Make sure you are using that other fifty percent wisely. What is most important is to pay yourself first. As I said, the initial item on the expense list is your name. That means you need to carve out a set amount each month, even if it's only fifty or one hundred dollars, to start with. Increase it when you can."

"Seems like there won't be anything left over."

Victoria didn't respond to Ally's comment, but went on to make her point. "Make sure you consider all expenditures that are out of the ordinary, like wedding gifts or birthday presents."

"But, I have a lifestyle to maintain. This seems so difficult."

Victoria sat back. While Victoria was not about to tolerate Ally's complaining, Ally caught herself falling back into a self-destructive attitude. This type of thinking was not going to get her where she wanted to go.

Victoria knew that this was not the time to take a confrontational stance with Ally. A scolding approach never worked to steer change; in fact, it usually fueled the feelings of defiance. She had gone through that with her niece several years ago. Her niece was stuck in a bind but when Victoria pointed out all the negatives about her behavior, her niece refused to listen to anything she said after that. Instead of heading down that non-productive path again, Victoria sympathized and attempted to facilitate change from Ally's point of view.

"This is a struggle for you, isn't it?"

"Uh-huh."

"I understand. It will be difficult for now because you're still not making much money. Are you sure you're ready for change now? You know, as the years go by and you can increase your salary, it will be easier. Once you make this a regular habit, it will feel good. After a few months, when you have some money saved up, you can set small goals for yourself. You don't want to be stuck now do you?"

Victoria tried to play on Ally's personal aspirations. "You seem so ready to change. From what I've heard you say, you want to have the security of an emergency fund, right?"

"Yes."

"And you want to be free from your credit card debt, right?"

"Yes."

Victoria continued reminding Ally of all the reasons why the changes were in her best interest. "And, you want to be able to make your own life choices, right?"

"Yes, I do." Ally heard herself answering the same questions she had wrestled with previously. Finally, she said "I'm ready to change." She smiled when she realized how Victoria had steered the conversation.

"Good. That's what I thought." Victoria knew it would work. By reminding Ally what her internal motivations were for making behavioral changes, Victoria reinforced the intentions.

"To avoid straying from your plan, make sure your plan includes activities that are inexpensive. What I mean by that is minimum activity spending. Instead of going out to dinner, have dinner at home and then go to the movies with friends. If they are meeting for drinks, meet them a little after the arranged time to reduce your time spent buying high-priced drinks. You have to convert your entire lifestyle to align with your goals."

"What other suggestions do you have?"

"Try to keep as little cash as possible in your wallet. That's not permission to overuse your credit cards; it means that the more cash you have, the more cash you are likely to spend. If you keep your cash in possession to a minimum, you will keep more money in your bank account. ATM withdrawals are the death of budgets."

"True," Ally said as she absorbed the new thoughts.

"You've taken the first step by lowering your rent expense. Use your commuting time to improve your working skills. Read, read, and read some more.

"So let's look at your updated goals."

1. Transfer fifty dollars or more to savings every payday
2. Bring (healthy) lunch to work every day
3. Pay off credit cards by four hundred dollars per month with money saved from rent
4. Fund employer retirement accounts
5. ~~Look for a more affordable (studio) apartment~~
6. Read one financial planning book

"You've already knocked one goal off the list. And it allows you to be able to have an additional four hundred dollars a month to work with."

"I have to admit, I still have some ambivalence about doing this. It feels very uncomfortable right now because I'm starting with nothing. Everything seems to be a struggle. Is it like this for everyone? Why do I have to feel like I'll never be able to do this?"

"Let's stop at this point. I think you have some concepts to digest. Keep your intentions at the forefront of your mind every day. That will keep you focused. Whenever you feel lost in the process, write down your ultimate goals and repeat them to yourself. Monitor the gains and don't fuel the negatives."

HOW BAD CAN IT GET?

By the end of the summer, Ally was doing fairly well adjusting to her new self-imposed rules. Sometimes, though, it still felt strange and she needed to reach out to Victoria to discuss her ambivalence.

"My friends are out having fun without a care in the world. Why can't I do the same?"

"It all comes down to altering your money mindset. It takes discipline, and yes, it feels uncomfortable to have to change financial habits. Most people feel unease when they have to change any habits. Overeating is a similar overindulgence. How do you think people feel when they have to stop overeating? It doesn't feel good. But sooner or later, their overindulgence threatens their health and they have to cut back. The same situation happens with money. Each time we talk, I'm giving you the steps to take. But what you don't think about is what your life might be like if you aren't cautious."

Ally looked a little spooked by that and braced herself for what Victoria was about to say. She wondered how bad it could be.

Victoria began. "Do you see people who never seem to get anywhere no matter how hard they try? They are always bitter and think that the world is against them. That bitterness invades everything they do and their relationships. It creates acrimony between spouses, jealousy among friends, and belligerence toward employers. These people feel out of control and that they have to settle. These individuals go with the flow, reluctantly.

"Constant debt creates stress from the lingering burden. Sometimes debts snowball and could take years to pay off. You don't want to be in a constant debt cycle. That means that someone holds something over you and will be relentless until you are done paying up.

"You won't have housing options that you're comfortable with. If you don't save up for your own home, you'll always be paying rent. That's OK if you don't suffer a hardship, like a job loss or a pay cut. If you experience a setback you might have to move back in with your parents. You wouldn't want that, would you? I've seen this happen to adult children many times. Then, you won't have your privacy. If you do stay in an apartment, that might not be terrible, but circumstances may not always be in your favor. Noisy neighboring tenants and poor services are inevitable. Your landlord could raise the rent at any time. You may lose heat, electricity, and water, and have no control over the services. It may be too hot or too cold. If you're not on the first floor, you might have to walk up flights of stairs. This may seem trivial until you have to haul groceries.

"You might not be able to make choices in your medical care. Some employers don't have adequate coverage or may pass the majority of the cost along to the employees. Some treatments may not be adequately covered by the medical plan offered to you and you may not be able to afford the out-of-pocket costs. Delaying or forgoing medical care is detrimental to your health.

"Women who don't make their own choices often live with a controlling husband. They have to ask for permission from their husband to make a purchase. If the husband says no, they have to live without. Gradually, the husband controls all the finances and requires approval for everything from clothing purchases to use of the family car. Very often, the husband allows himself his own pleasures but denies his wife. This creates tremendous discord. The most common reasons for irreconcilable differences between spouses are money issues."

"That would never happen to me," Ally said.

"You might think so. When women don't get involved in the marital finances, they are exposing themselves to tremendous risk of being controlled or left with no resources. In the mildest form, a husband slowly takes over all decisions, expressing disapproval and anger when a wife makes a purchase without consulting him. In what is known as Financial Domestic Abuse, the husband uses the financial circumstances as a form of control to ensure that his wife is dependent on him. That leaves no opportunities for leaving the relationship because the wife has no means of her own to support herself, no money even for transportation to vacate."

"That's terrible." Ally was shocked to hear such a thing.

"There are three forms of financial abuse identified by social work professor Judy Postmus, director of the Center on Violence Against Women and Children. Control, exploitation, and sabotage. Another version of financial abuse is financial infidelity."

"What's that?"

"Financial infidelity occurs when one spouse incurs a huge amount of debt without informing the other spouse. It could be credit card purchases or it could be taking on a second mortgage. Regardless of the form, the spouse has burdened the relationship with financial strain."

Ally let this simmer in her thoughts. She couldn't imagine people doing this to each other.

"These situations can take many years to overcome. The resulting options are paying off the debt or settling with a cancellation of indebtedness. In many cases, paying off the debt means not being able to save or afford a comfortable lifestyle. Settling with creditors with a cancellation of indebtedness affects the person's credit rating for many years—again, limiting lifestyle choices. What most people also don't know is that the amount of debt cancelled or forgiven is reported as income. The person will get a 1099 at year-end."

Ally hated to think where that went. It seemed like bad money problems quickly escalate to worse money problems.

"Working to pay off a huge debt or having to start over after many years of working and saving is not a good position to be in. Individuals in their forties and fifties are left in these circumstances without much hope. Job opportunities are not as plentiful for highly experienced workers. Jobs become competitive, and technology advances replace jobs. Personal circumstances may not allow these individuals to pursue new careers and those limits affect their retirement years.

"The third category of financial abuse involves sabotaging the victim's ability to work—disrupting child care or transportation, or harassing the victim at work until she's let go or too embarrassed to show up. That is the ultimate in not having control over your life. These women allow someone to dictate what their standard of living is and how happy their life will be. Never take the ignorant approach. Some women think that because they're not good at numbers, they don't need to have an awareness of the family's finances. Some aren't motivated to understand what they need to know. They refuse to make decisions, afraid to make the wrong choice. Some hesitate when making choices, leaving their spouses to act on their own. Always know your financial situation, make your own decisions, and maintain tight control over your personal finances. Protecting what you have is as important as earning it."

Ally knew she never wanted to be the kind of woman who couldn't make her own decisions and had no control over her finances. She was listening intently, taking it all in, and also becoming familiar with the idea of financial abuse, something she hadn't even known existed before now.

Victoria saw the impact her words had on Ally. "Just to give you additional background, consider the latest information. According to a recent report, *Silent Weapons: Domestic Violence and Financial Abuse*, thirty-nine percent of women say they have taken steps to protect themselves from financial abuse, including thirty-three percent of millennial women."

"Millennial women! Why, that's me and my friends, isn't it? How can women born in the '80s and '90s be as dependent on their spouses as their mothers or grandmothers were? Why are fewer than half of millennial women aware of the possibility of financial abuse?"

"Think about your own story, Ally, and how your parents dealt with their finances and how limited your financial education was. More than half of Americans say their parents have never talked to them about keeping their personal finances managed and secure. Americans also acknowledge that they wouldn't necessarily recognize the warning signs for a friend who is being abused or know what to do to help."

Ally wondered who she knew that might be in a financially abusive relationship. According to the statistics Victoria shared, she was sure to know someone in those circumstances, even if she didn't see the warning signs. Maybe she would now.

Victoria saw that the statistics she had quoted had made an impression on Ally and decided to give her more to think about.

"Sixty-five percent of survey respondents don't believe that their family or friends would know if they were in a financially abusive relationship and seventy percent can't say they would know how to help them. Despite viewing domestic violence as a serious problem, Americans are not talking about the issue. Only one in three says they have discussed the issue with friends or family. What do you think of those survey results?"

"Pretty scary."

"That's right. It is scary."

"Now that I understand the issue, I can see that my friends are headed in the wrong direction. I wonder if they'll ever get on the right track. They're so scattered right now. I realize we're young but it seems like they just can't get a clue. I try to talk to some of my friends about these conversations with you and they aren't even interested."

"That's too bad."

"I think that's enough for today; you've given me so much to think about. Thanks for enlightening me. Exploitation, sabotage, financial infidelity—I never gave much thought to those extreme control issues, and while it's all so disturbing, it's also really good to know."

CREDIT

Ally decided to add to her list of goals.

1. Transfer fifty dollars to savings every payday
2. Bring healthy lunch to work
3. Pay off credit cards with money saved from rent
4. Fund employer retirement accounts
5. ~~Look for a more affordable (studio) apartment~~
6. Read one financial planning book
7. Check credit score

The next time she saw Victoria, she wanted to continue discussing what she needed to do to avoid ending up in a bad situation. She also wanted to learn about how credit scores worked.

"I liked hearing about negative situations," she told Victoria. "Not because I want it to make me depressed, but because it helps keep me mindful of what I need to focus on. It helps me gain insight into situations that I know nothing of and wouldn't see coming. These are topics that I don't think about on a regular basis. How else could money situations negatively affect our lives?"

"You know, if you're not careful, it's not a far drop from where you are to financial devastation. Keep that in mind. There are many people who are one life event away from a financial disaster. One poor decision could cost tens of thousands of dollars, especially when there's a lack of insurance. Lack of adequate medical coverage, a bad investment decision, lack of income replacement in the event of a disability—there are so many variations of caution."

"So, insurance is major. Got it."

"Let's look at some hidden costs. Your ability to support your lifestyle will affect the kind of car you will be able to afford and I don't mean because of the cost of the car. The monthly cost of any car you choose should be doubled to account for the cost of insurance. Car insurance is costly for nice cars. You might be able to afford the car you want, but not the insurance. You'll want to be able to afford the insurance for the car that you choose."

Ally was glad she didn't need a car right now to commute to her job or to visit her parents or Victoria. Her social life was in the city, so she was fine without a car at present but would keep in mind what Victoria said when the time was right.

"How will you feel when you want to take a vacation that you can't afford? If your credit limit is maxed out and you don't have anything saved, you'll be staying home. When you handcuff yourself with debt, you may not be able to enjoy a nice vacation for many years."

Ally wanted to be on the intelligent side of those decisions, not left behind.

"When you don't make your own choices, someone else will make them for you. That's a given. Individuals stuck in a poor financial situation have to settle for limited choices. It can be incredibly frustrating and leads to resentment. Remember that no one has your best interest in mind but you.

"You will enjoy your life much more if you have no debt. Delaying gratification is part of the solution. Don't you want to be able to take nice vacations and buy your friends and family nice things? You have the ability to do all that, and you deserve it. It might feel like everything is difficult now, but stick to your plan, chip away at what you must accomplish, and you'll have peace of mind and fewer worries.

"You will not believe the satisfaction that financial security will bring you. You will eventually have too many choices, but that's a good problem to have. Work now at making the right decisions. Once your habits are established, it will feel like second nature. You will develop contentment once you see your savings and investment balances. It won't feel like deprivation.

"Let's move on and talk about your credit card accounts."

"Yes. What should I know about credit?"

"Credit is a great aspect of our lives. Merchandisers are willing to provide the ability to purchase goods and services before they are actually paid for. This allows consumers to obtain what they need without having immediate funds. Consumers may apply this arrangement for convenience or for needed goods and services in an emergency. The downside is that credit card companies want you to stay in debt forever. They are hoping that the borrower will only pay the minimum amount and accrue interest on the unpaid principal balance. A continuous monthly payment gives them a constant source of income. When only the minimum payment is made, the credit card company continually recalculates interest to keep the balance high. It may take years to pay off the entire principal—years that are valuable.

"To give you some perspective of how precarious this all is, it would take three hundred seventy months to pay off a two-thousand-dollar balance at an eighteen percent annual rate. You would end up paying thousands of dollars in interest."

Ally's eyes widened. "That's way too long. What's the best plan to get rid of my credit card debt? I have three large accounts and two smaller store accounts."

"To get started with your paydown plan, pay the minimum on all cards, paying more on the one with the highest interest rate. Continue doing that until all the balances are paid off. Then limit your spending to only one card. You don't need a store card for every store that you buy from. Their ten percent initial discount can be enticing but it's not worth it to you to have an open line of credit of several thousand dollars for several accounts."

Victoria waited for that to register, then went on. "For the cards that you stop using, don't cancel the accounts, simply stop using them. Better yet, cut them up."

"What other strategies should I keep in mind?"

"Always pay on time. Be diligent about paying off your debts. Your credit score will be determined by your credit history. This means that your ability to pay your debts will guarantee the lowest possible rate of interest on loans when you need to purchase a home or a car."

"How did you get started with credit cards?"

"My own personal experience with credit cards began when a department store gave me my first credit card. I was dying to use it and actually felt lucky that they had granted me credit. I bought a pair of blue jeans for twenty dollars. When I came home from the store, I put five dollars on my shelf. For the next three weeks, I put five dollars on my shelf. When the bill came, I put the twenty dollars in the bank and wrote a check to pay for the twenty-dollar pants. It's really that simple. On a larger scale, having the money up front before making purchases is the smartest way to ensure that you will pay the entire bill."

Ally appreciated how Victoria was able to simplify her explanations so anyone could understand them, and waited for more of Victoria's good advice.

"Many people think that allowing a minimum payment is the store's way of being nice to them. If they only have to make the minimum payment, everything will work itself out. Newsflash: the credit card company is not your friend! While we're talking about credit cards, you need to know your credit score."

"How do I find my credit score?"

"There are several online websites that will provide you with a copy of your credit score. You can go to freecreditscore.com, Experian, Equifax, or TransUnion.

"Make sure you understand your score. It will determine if you're eligible for a car loan or home loan and dictates the lowest interest rate you will be eligible for. It can also affect your ability to get a job or get promoted. And it affects your insurance rates."

"Really? It affects insurance rates?"

"Yes, think about it. Your ability to manage credit is very closely tied to your propensity to be disciplined or reckless with your decisions. Most people who are careless with their money tend to be careless in other areas of their lives. By definition, insurance is a transfer of risk. When the insurance company takes on a person's risk, it tries to get a sense of how responsible that person is. Responsibility for debts and decision-making skills are very closely related. The cost of not being disciplined is quite alarming. According to Credit Karma, bad credit can cost you up to *two hundred thirty thousand dollars more* in interest payments over a lifetime than someone with a good credit score."

"Wow! That's crazy. Over a lifetime, that's an enormous amount of money. So, what's a good score number?"

"Higher than seven hundred fifty is ideal. Bad credit is considered having a score less than six hundred forty."

"What's the best way to get and maintain a good credit score?"

"Well, that's elementary. Pay your bills on time. Check your credit score periodically and make sure that vendors have reported your transactions properly. Keep your credit usage well below your maximum limit. That would be using no more than thirty percent of your maximum allowed credit. It would be good to limit the number of credit accounts that you have. Your ability to manage your available credit is as important as your payment history."

"How have you managed credit?"

"In addition to my first store card where I paid for the twenty-dollar jeans by saving five dollars a week, I had opened a number of other store accounts as well as Master-

Card and Visa accounts. Back then, everything was paid by check and mailed—there were no online payment methods. It was so cumbersome writing all those checks, stuffing the envelopes, and needing stamps, that I limited myself to using only two accounts. I realize how convenient it is to pay bills online now but it doesn't make any sense to use multiple credit accounts at the same time. Unless you are making a large purchase from a store that is offering an interest-free financing period, you should be able to stick to one Visa or MasterCard account. Do you think you can do that?"

"Yes. I'll stop using four or five different accounts."

"Another thing. If they increase your limit, call them and tell them to keep it at the level that it was. When they increase your maximum level of credit, another potential lender perceives that as a possibility to max out your borrowings, taking on unmanageable levels of debt. If they think you will take on too much debt, they run the risk of not being paid back after extending credit to you."

"I see."

"I remember getting a letter from one of my credit card companies. They knew I only had a few years' worth of credit history behind me. But they were notifying me that they recognized me as a person who managed credit in a responsible manner. I was very proud of that and made sure it stayed that way. I'm certain that that's what helped me buy my first house."

"I've seen the cute commercials where they're advertising the free credit reports. I don't fully understand why that's important."

"Make sure to check your credit report at least once a year. You don't want to find out that there's an error or that someone has opened accounts in your name. You can get a free report at annualcreditreport.com. Federal law allows you to ensure that the information on all of your credit reports is correct and up to date.

"If your credit score is less than seven hundred fifty, take steps immediately to increase it. Add that to your goal list. It can take years to mitigate a damaged credit history. If it's not stellar now, at least you can make sure it won't continue for a prolonged period of time."

"What can people do if their credit score is low?"

"One option is to apply for a secured credit card."

"I've never heard of that."

"Many people have never heard of it. Used properly, it can be a great way to restore an unhealthy credit rating."

"How does it work?"

"A secured credit card requires a cash collateral amount as a deposit. It's usually three hundred dollars or five hundred dollars as a minimum. The cash amount becomes the limit for the account. It's like a self-imposed credit balance. You may be able to add to the limit by depositing additional money."

"How does it help the credit score?"

"If the card issuer reports activity to the credit bureaus, good behavior will quickly be reflected in your credit rating. The only danger is if they have it flagged as a secured account. That would hurt a report."

"How would I get a secured credit card?"

"You can look at bankrate.com's list of issuers."

"Is there a catch to doing this?"

"They might impose very high fees. You may have to pay a fee but you don't want it to completely diminish your balance. You also don't want to be roped into paying for insurance fees or any other add-ons."

"I don't think I need to do that now but it's good to know."

"It's very helpful to people who need to restore credit after having been turned down for loans. In some cases, the credit score can be increased from less than six hundred to more than seven hundred in a short period of time. In drastic situations, the best combination is a secured credit card combined with significant paydowns of outstanding balances."

Ally wasn't sure of her credit score and started to look worried.

"Don't think of your financial corrections as a hardship. It may seem a bit austere at first, but you'll adjust. Keep reminding yourself that you're providing for your future lifestyle and setting yourself up for financial success. In your later years, you'll realize that you didn't miss much by not constantly spending."

Ally sat back and realized there was work to do. "I'm going to look up some of this information at the library and get a full understanding. So many people are at a disadvantage in not being fully aware. In our plastic money society, this is such a universal topic and everyone should be informed. Some people I know think that money comes from an ATM machine. They don't understand that you work for it first and then need to control spending habits. I want you to know that I've gained so much confidence with my new insight."

RELYING ON YOURSELF

The demand for Victoria's monologue sessions had expanded to where participants were requesting scheduled dates in advance. Victoria hosted this session in her home. The gathering was a small, familiar crowd. Ally noted that some of the women brought their daughters with them. She overheard the moms telling their daughters to pay attention.

Don't ever rely on anyone to give you what you want. Why would you do that? Too many people think someone else will take care of their needs and wants. Young women think that some Prince Charming will come along and rescue them. Young men think that they will find a young lady with a wealthy family or lucrative family business. Both young men and women think that their parents will take care of them forever.

Many young women who don't want to make the effort to improve themselves think that the way out is to become hitched to a man. That may or may not work. If it does, it's great. If it doesn't, the downside is steep. The security and lifestyle in the beginning may be there but that can all be taken away in an instant. The person who controls the purse strings makes the decisions.

Why would you want someone making decisions for your life? Do you want someone telling you where and how you will live? You need to make your own decisions regardless of what your spouse or family provides you with. You will never have autonomy and will never make your own decisions if someone else controls money that will support your needs. Divorce is common, infidelity is common. Don't leave your security in someone else's hands because if your situation turns, no one cares about you but you.

Even if you do find Prince Charming, he may not be wealthy. He may even have debt. Be careful of your choice of spouse. Your spouse may shower you with gifts but debt may be mounting without your knowledge.

Never lie to yourself about your money situation. Think very carefully about what you are spending before you spend it.

Many husbands and fathers want their families to be proud of them. They provide and spend, making it look effortless. I know of some wives and daughters who found out too late how much the patriarch owed to creditors. The man of the family maintained a façade of wealth. It made him feel important and kept the family from worrying. Little did the family know what the real situation was. Sometimes they didn't find out until dad died.

It's not wise to rely on an inheritance either. Mom and dad may be planning expensive vacations or planning to purchase their retirement home. Worse yet, some elderly people accumulate debt that they cannot pay off. Many retired people are bored and engage in unhealthy spending. Gambling and shopping become habit-forming for some older folks. Have you seen all the retirees getting off buses in Atlantic City? Some have not only squandered their life savings, but have built up debt, even remortgaging their homes. This is doubly compounded by not having an income to pay off the debt.

Bottom line: always have your own. Earn your own money. Support yourself. No one can take that away from you. You will never have to rely on anyone and will value yourself and your achievements.

Everyone should be self-sufficient—everyone. It doesn't matter who you are or what you do. Everyone needs to attain a minimum level of self-sustenance. That means you pay your own rent or mortgage, buy your own food, pay for your own car and insurance, and buy your own luxuries. When you take something from someone else, you end up paying one way or another. Parents lay terrible guilt on their children. Possessions from a spouse can be claimed back in a divorce settlement.

There is nothing sadder than seeing people who have hit on hard times and thought they could bank on steady employment, inheritances, property valuations, or lawsuit settlements. Those are the people who have to severely downsize when they have no last resort. You do not want to be stuck without resources or choices. Cover yourself—always!

Victoria asked if anyone had questions and the women began a lively discussion. Everyone knew someone who had been stuck in a financial bind. Some situations could have been prevented; some could have been mitigated by planning for the unknown. Regardless, stress was involved.

Ally observed how beneficial it was to have an open discussion. The women who spoke up displayed some discomfort talking about money issues, but they were visibly composed afterward. It was cathartic to talk and listen.

Ally knew she would be seeing this group again.

FIND FREE SERVICES

Ally went straight to the online catalog at the library. She entered "financial planning" and found the section. Then she went to work. She took some financial planning books off the shelf and sat down with her notebook. She was going to start doing some serious reading and take notes. After an hour, she checked out two books.

Not only was the library good for free books, it also offered many other money-saving options. She noticed the DVDs. Instead of spending money on going to movies, she could check out a DVD and stay at home. She saw the magazines. Now, instead of paying the newsstand price or for a tablet subscription, she could come to the library to read. That would be a good substitute for spending her leisure time when she might be tempted to go to the mall. Ally thought of how the library was a much better alternative than going to a bookstore and spending a ton of money. This was a significant step in the right direction. She was always buying books. During her recent move, she had lugged all the boxes of accumulated books and realized how many she didn't finish.

Ally picked up a newsletter on the way out and was amazed at all the activities the library offered. Five-dollar yoga classes, free seminars, museum passes, art events, résumé help, even online GMAT testing.

The newsletter noted the library's website, which included a wealth of resources. There were books to download, an online catalog alert service, and an online research service. She noted the Business/Finance research link. That would come in handy when she wanted to research investments.

It was time to take advantage of these free—yes, *free*—services.

When Ally arrived home she turned her computer on and went to creditkarma.com. After downloading the reports, she reviewed the entries carefully. Her credit score was six hundred ten; not as healthy as she would like it to be. OK, it was in need of some help. It wasn't terrible, but she didn't want it to stay there or go any lower. She made a note to talk to Victoria about some alternate ways to improve her credit score.

ALLY AND AMY

Ally had become friends with her coworker Amy over the past six months. They didn't know each other well at first, but when they worked on an assignment together, they realized how much they had in common. Amy was almost the total opposite of Taylor. Ally could have a complete conversation with her, not like the frenetic responses she got from Taylor. Amy had a sensible air about her, and both she and Amy had career aspirations. Amy was one year older and newly engaged.

One day when they went out to lunch, Amy brought up how concerned she was about being able to pay for her wedding. Ally mentioned that she was getting her finances together and talked about her "coach," Victoria.

"Really? What kinds of things do you talk about? For as long as I can remember, I've always had money problems. Since my parents' divorce, my mom always played the poor, abandoned single mom."

"I didn't have good role models either," Ally said, "but Victoria is giving me all kinds of advice on how to manage my money and make plans for the future. That's the reason I left my high-rent apartment. I don't know what I was thinking, living in the middle of Manhattan."

"That's such an adjustment to make."

"I know, but so worth it. Now, I can pay off my credit card debt."

"That's good. I'll be racking up some bills while we plan our wedding."

Ally had an idea. "You know, I was thinking about different ways to avoid spending. Would you mind it if I used you as my hotline, like if I'm about to make an expensive purchase, I can call you and you can talk me out of it?"

"Kind of like an addiction sponsor?" They both laughed. As silly as it sounded, it was similar. "That's fine as long as you don't call me in the middle of the night. Can you start with a text and if I can call you back, I will?"

"That would really be great. I promise I won't be a stalker, and I'll do the same for you."

Amy nodded in agreement. "Let me tell you, I really need the help. It's tough to keep within a spending budget when planning for a wedding. I went to look for a dress thinking I wouldn't go over one thousand dollars. After going to several shops, I rationalized spending up to two thousand dollars. By the time I bought the dress, it was about twenty-five hundred dollars."

"Wow. That's expensive."

"It's really beautiful but I think I got a little carried away. That's what happens when you get caught up in all the excitement. Now we have to limit other things because of how much we want to put toward buying a house."

"I know how that happens. That's why I'm stuck paying off credit card debt. But my mentor is showing me how it's possible to pay everything down and save at the same time."

They walked back to work, both feeling positive about the pact they had made. It solidified their friendship. Talking finances with friends wasn't always easy, Ally thought. *At least I found someone who will support my new mentality.*

Ally started reading one of her financial management books that evening. Every author has a different way of developing and presenting the material. This author emphasized budgeting and personal financial statements. Ally glanced at the typical budgeting spreadsheet and was glad she was past that. She could skip that section. She wanted to stick to her mini-goal of reading at least five pages per day.

Her other two mini-goals were to carry as little cash as possible and to write down all her purchases to keep track of her spending. She committed to entering the spending in her notebook and reviewing it at the end of the week.

BASIC FINANCIAL TERMS

Ally looked at some of the terms in one of the financial planning books that she had picked up at the library. Income statements, balance sheets, compound interest … what did all this mean? She would have to ask Victoria or look up the definitions on her own.

It was a lot to take in, but she remembered what Victoria had said—one step at a time. Not to get overwhelmed and give up. Ally took out her notebook and made a list of the terms that she wanted to learn more about.

Balance sheet. Ally did a Google search for "balance sheet." Investopedia explained it as "A financial statement that summarizes a company's assets, liabilities, and shareholder's equity at a specific point in time." *Not sure that applies. I'm not a company.* Before she was about to give up, she tried again. She changed the search to "personal balance sheet" and looked at *moneymanagement.org* and found information about determining net worth. That sounded better. Ally read the definition: "A balance sheet calculates your net worth by comparing your financial assets (what you own) with your financial liabilities (what you owe)." *Well, that should be easy. I don't own anything and owe lots of money.* She continued reading. "Don't be discouraged if your net worth is negative—

keep in mind that this should be an accurate depiction of your financial situation. Setting goals is much easier once you know what your current net worth is."

The website listed all the information that was needed to calculate personal net worth—cash in bank accounts, investments, IRAs, 401(k)s, and the value of personal items owned. All amounts owed would be listed as negative items. That would include school loans, car loans, mortgages, and credit card balances. Subtotals would be calculated at the bottom of each column.

That doesn't seem so hard. Ally took a template from an Internet site and loaded everything into Excel. She entered the date that she worked on it. It wasn't much to brag about now but it was something to go over the next time she saw Victoria, and Ally felt as though she had accomplished something by researching it on her own.

When Ally went over her balance sheet with Victoria, Victoria was thrilled that Ally had taken it upon herself to not only look up the financial terms and educate herself, but to go so far as to populate a worksheet.

"Nice work, Allison! Today's balance sheet is your starting point. It may seem discouraging now, but if you use this as a benchmark, you can chart your progress. See where your liabilities are with your credit card debt? You want to focus on those areas and reduce them. We've already talked about this, so you have that point down. After you have some of your liabilities reduced, you can focus on increasing the asset side."

"How can I use this to measure my progress?"

"Take inventory twice a year. You can measure progress by increasing assets. You want to increase your assets owned in a wise manner. What I mean by that is, be sure to purchase assets that will last for many years."

"What's the best to focus on?"

"A home and a car are where people spend the most. Let's take a car as an example. This asset is probably the most important one to think about. I recommend that you buy only what you can afford and make sure that you keep it for many years. You want to be able to take advantage of the value of the vehicle. Too many people trade in their cars too soon and then obtain a new one. If this is done more frequently than three years, money is being wasted. Not only that, a car is an asset that depreciates as soon as it leaves the dealer's lot."

"What do you mean?"

"A car can lose half of its value within the first four years, maybe more depending on the mileage."

"So, how long should a car be kept?"

"A car should be kept until the wheels fall off. That might sound ridiculous, but if a car is properly maintained, it should last at least ten years. And don't forget about insurance. With the cost of a new car comes the insurance. The maintenance on an owned car should be below the total of the new car payments plus insurance."

"How about leasing?"

"Leasing should be avoided, if possible. A leased car is like paying rent for the use of the car. Also, a down payment on a leased car should be as close to zero as possible. The down payment on a leased car will not be recovered if the car is stolen or totaled in an accident."

"I didn't know that."

"Most people don't. The down payment may initially reduce the monthly lease payment but that money is basically lost. If it reduces the value of the buyout at the end of the lease, it might be worth it. If a car is leased, the best way to maintain the value is to buy the car from the dealer after the lease period ends."

"How long a car loan should I request?"

"As far as car loans goes, the loan duration should be kept to a minimum, such as three years. Five- or six-year car loans should be avoided. I've recently seen car loans advertised for seventy-two or ninety-six months. That's just absurd. You know, my first new car wasn't very pretty. In fact, it was pretty ugly. However, it had a low monthly payment and was great on gas mileage. I soon realized that the low payment allowed me to save money and enjoy myself. When the loan payments ended, I bought the car and kept it for eight more years. Leasing was not attractive to me because there are other pitfalls as well."

"Like what?"

"People forget there could also be a mileage limit and damage fee at the end of the lease period and they can get stuck with unexpected charges. No one will admit to incurring these expenses. They will brag about their shiny new leased car, though."

"I know," Ally said, rolling her eyes. "One thing I worry about with car buying is the negotiation. It always sounds tricky."

"Let me suggest this. Get all your facts together about the car you want. Include details on all the options and calculate the price you will pay. Then call a dealership and ask if they can provide you with what you want at your price. I know people who have done this over the phone. They don't let a salesperson decide what they want and what they will pay. If the dealer tries to sway the situation or won't meet your request, you move on."

"You can buy a car that way?" Ally said.

"Yes. This buying method is a perfect example of how when you don't make your own choices, someone else will. With car buying, the salesperson will gladly decide what the buyer should be paying, eventually pulling an uninformed buyer into the deep end of the pool. Before the buyer knows it, she will be paying for things that she didn't know existed and will most likely have a higher monthly payment. It's so easy to get information from the Internet now. Use that to your advantage. A car purchase is the largest cost you will incur besides a home. Invest the time in getting your money's worth."

CASH FLOW STATEMENT

"Let's move on. You should understand what a cash flow statement is. You'll see that it's closely related to your budget."

"OK." Ally was ready.

"A cash flow statement is an accounting of income and expenses over a period of time. By recording every incoming dollar and outgoing dollar, the uses of cash are clearly laid out. On the simple side of a cash flow statement you would enter your income, such as your salary, bonuses, and other income, earned or unearned. Earned income is personal service income, like your job. Unearned income is interest and dividends. Then you would record all uses of cash—all cash outflows for amounts spent."

"Seems basic enough. Does it get more complicated than that?"

"To be more detailed, you can categorize your uses of cash by using the following headings: operating, capital, and financing. Operating activities represent the daily functions of the household. These expenses can be further bifurcated into discretionary spending and nondiscretionary spending. Nondiscretionary spending represents items that cannot be avoided. This would include rent or mortgage payments, food, taxes, and utilities.

"Discretionary spending represents items that you choose to purchase—entertainment items, impulse buys, and other nonessential items that are not necessary but provide personal pleasure. You would want to determine how much you are spending in each category. If you saw that you were spending too much in the discretionary category, then that gives you a clue to where to cut back, right?"

Victoria didn't wait for an answer. "Capital spending is for household items that provide a long-term benefit. Kitchen appliances are a good example of this category. Kitchen appliances are big-ticket items that are not purchased each year. They provide benefits for household use for many years. Another example of this is furniture. Some furniture can be useful for a lifetime. These types of expenditures are considered a form of investment. One other very important item is the section of the cash flow statement that segregates financing activities."

"What does the financing section represent?"

"The financing cash flow activity indicates differences in the household's debt level. Increases in debt are considered an increase in cash flow. This may seem counterintuitive, but I'll explain. If you buy a car for cash, that entire amount reduces your cash available. But if you take a car loan and increase your debt by taking the loan, you have theoretically increased your cash available. Does that make sense? If you paid off a car loan in a lump sum, you would reduce your cash flow by that entire amount."

"Oh, I see."

"You make decisions on how you spend your cash flow every day but I think you should understand the concepts to make better decisions. Your purchases are either for current living needs or future living needs. Examples of cash spent on current living needs are for items that provide short-term fulfillment, such as eating out. Cash spent on future living needs is put into accounts that will cover future expenses; for example, in retirement. Your decision to not spend today provides you with a cushion for future uses. It's not that you are denying yourself, as you are only denying yourself temporarily. If you look at it that way, saving doesn't seem so difficult."

Ally jumped in. "To be honest, retirement seems like such a long way away. And I have so many things that I need now."

Victoria understood. "I know. Try to think of more immediate reasons. Besides retirement savings, a future use of cash would be for a down payment on a condo. That's something you would consider now, right?"

"Yes, I guess so."

"There's no reason why you can't start a separate pool of money to put toward your own condo. Just remember, Ally, be careful when estimating expenditures. I know I've mentioned this before but many people forget about expenses like haircuts, birthday presents, wedding presents, and Christmas. These aren't typical monthly expenses; they require a significant amount of cash and can easily dent a budget out of proportion. A very common mistake with budgeting is the omission of these recurring items. Also, you don't want to be the person who says, "*How could I be in overdraft when I still have checks left?*"

THE CAREER SESSION

Summer was kicking in and it was getting warm. Ally's mom called to set a date for the family's annual summer trip.

"Are you still speaking with Victoria? How is she?"

"She's great, Mom. I'm learning so much from her. She's so smart and has wonderful advice."

"That's great. I guess it's easier to get money advice from someone who's more objective than a family member—like your mom."

"I understand you did things the way you felt was right. Family dynamics played a big role, I guess."

"That's true. Once you have a family of your own, you'll understand. Well, as long as you're learning and moving ahead, I'm happy for you. I only want what's best for you. The world has changed so much now and there are opportunities that weren't available to me when I was your age. What is she teaching you?"

"So much. I'll tell you more over the summer vacation."

"Send Victoria my regards."

"OK. Bye, Mom."

Ally left her apartment and headed to Victoria's for a three-month check-in.

Victoria had finger sandwiches and appetizers set up. She couldn't wait to see Ally. It had been three months since she had begun coaching her, and Ally was off to a great start by making lists and starting a savings plan. By now, some of her procedures should be well underway, with Ally taking serious steps toward her financial goals.

Ally arrived on time and full of confidence. She couldn't wait to show Victoria her notebook. She was hungry and the little sandwiches looked delicious, but she was so excited to share her progress that she forgot about her hunger pangs and grabbed her notebook, library books, and bank statements.

"How *are* you? This lunch looks great but do I have news for you! Here's my bank statement. I was able to increase my savings to three hundred dollars per month. And I'm reading these great financial planning books, and I found all these free or low-cost things to take advantage of by going to the local library. I'm also paying three hundred fifty dollars per month toward my credit cards."

"That's great Allison. Tell me how you managed to increase your savings."

"It wasn't easy. I had to really focus on cutting corners. I started by bringing my lunch to work every day. I cook fresh meals on the weekends and started out wrapping sandwiches in aluminum foil. I did that for a few weeks but then invested in some good plastic lunch bowls and now take a sandwich and a side dish. I bring my own snacks so that I don't spend money in the overpriced vending machines. My snacks are also healthier and it keeps me from being tempted by the candy and cookie jars around the office."

"That's wonderful. What's going on at your job?"

"I was able to take on a separate project that came up, in addition to my own regular work. I fit everything in and the other manager is really pleased that I volunteered to help out. I wanted to spread my reach by working with other managers. I made sure my current manager was OK with it too. I don't want to step on anyone's toes or go beyond boundaries and risk offending someone."

"That's great! You'll find that your networking skills will really help you and it sounds like you're going about it the right way.

"Let's talk a little bit more about your career. You have an education. That's the best situation for you to be in. An education is something no one can take away from you. I know people who don't have an education because someone in their life told them they shouldn't go to college or finish high school. These messages are hard to unwind. When the message comes from parents, it's so embedded that it prevents them from even considering a degree. These young people shortchange their growth by not realizing their potential."

"You're right. I remember people in high school who had no direction."

"There are also college graduates who don't put their education to work for them," Victoria said. "They work in an unrelated field or don't expand on their undergraduate education. Some graduates don't get enough work experience related to their area of study. After a period of time, their degree isn't useful because they don't have the marketable skills that correspond to their education. Work experience is critical to building valuable career skills. That's what employers pay for.

"There's no greater waste of time and money than an education that's not put to use. Some people spend years earning a college education that their parents pay for and then decide that they don't like their career choice. Many careers that begin with obtaining a bachelor's degree require additional licenses or a master's degree to be competitive. I know accounting students who have not taken the CPA exam. They don't attempt it, thinking that it's too hard to study for. Unfortunately, accountants without a CPA license don't get very far in their career. For the first few years, everyone will be on the same level, but after a few years, those who earn the CPA license and gain valuable accounting experience will move on with their career, leaving the others behind. Accountants without a CPA license may not be competitive in the job market. Not having that license costs that college graduate many hundreds of thousands of dollars in compensation when all the years of a working career are taken into consideration. Same with law students. Law students who finish their college and law school education and don't take the bar exam are cutting off their opportunities."

"That seems foolish," Ally said. "I know people who seemed so serious in college but when they had to take serious action, like take a professional exam, they made excuses why they weren't interested in that career path."

"That seems counterintuitive. They are working to earn a degree in a certain field and then they pretend not to be interested in the career? I can't figure it out, but I've seen it happen also. The plain truth is that professional licenses are difficult and require effort. Sometimes it means taking the exams more than once and it pays to be persistent. Do everything you can to ensure that the best opportunities will be available to you."

"I'm on a straightforward career path right now, although there are some diversions I could consider," Ally said.

"What career goals do you have? You need to make your career work for you if you want it to provide you with the lifestyle you choose. Have you planned your income growth? This should be planned in tandem with your professional development. What training classes have you taken? How do you plan to maximize your career development?"

Ally understood that her career development was the key to affording her the lifestyle she wanted, plus financial security, and wondered what else she could do to advance her career.

Victoria knew that Ally had questions she could not yet articulate, and helped her out. "I know you have taken on new projects at work, and that's an important step. Can you volunteer for more projects? If your current job is a dead end, you need to look elsewhere for opportunities to continue your professional growth. Your skills must be marketable at all times. Your profession is your currency that you offer to the world. You'll be getting paid for your services for many years and your career will be your vehicle."

Ally thought about where her career was leading—and where she wanted to go. "There are a lot of unanswered questions related to my career," she said.

"I know. That's why I'm asking them all. I'm trying to convey to you that you're a multi-dimensional employee. Take advantage of all your dimensions and you'll grow faster than your colleagues."

"But how do I tackle all these issues?" Ally asked.

"First thing, don't get too complacent unless you are on the promotion fast track. What training can you take now? Does your employer offer tuition reimbursement for a master's degree in your field? This is an invaluable benefit. If it is offered, you need to take advantage of it. And if you're not promoted after you finish the degree, you need to consider moving on.

"Are you being paid fairly for your worth? Be determined to earn what you are worth. If you are being dismissed in your efforts where you currently are, let your employer know. If your employer doesn't care, you need to promote yourself. Translation: go out and get a higher-paying/higher-responsibility position. Another employer will surely appreciate your skills. Don't ever let anyone tell you that you can't increase your abilities and be paid more than what you are earning."

Ally was fascinated by the possibilities she hadn't even known to consider. *What a compelling topic. No one has ever taken the time to offer me career advice in this manner.* She didn't know which question to ask first.

"How do I get started?"

"When you're first starting out it's hard to see the big picture. What you really should do is map out where you are now and create a checklist of career-building skills. You should be working toward at least one goal per month."

"Can you help me create a roadmap?"

"Of course, but let's start with this discussion for now. You need to develop good working skills. Listen to instruction carefully, whether it comes from a manager, colleague, or customer. Make sure you have good instructions so you can meet expectations. Be mindful of deadlines and what your managers value. Your managers will always value you if you provide the assistance they need to help them do their jobs. If you make your manager's job easy, you'll develop trust. Understand that your reputation is built upon your actions. You want to be known as someone who can accomplish things, not be a burden. There's nothing wrong with expressing yourself, but don't turn into a complainer. You don't want to be known as someone who's difficult to work with. For every issue that frustrates you, develop a suggestion. Anyone can lay blame and criticize; it takes an insightful person to make suggestions and propose innovations. No manager wants a difficult employee, so make yourself as helpful as possible. Remember that there is no perfect employer. There's good and bad everywhere you work. If the good outweighs the bad, you're in the right place."

"Our managers never seem to appreciate us. They can be so critical at times and say inappropriate things to people."

"Some managers haven't been given the right training in working with people. They probably do appreciate you but need you to take the initiative. They may not be good at giving you the tools to get there and that creates an atmosphere of frustration on both sides. Some issues never get resolved and result in high turnover."

"Turnover is a big issue in some departments where I work. We share a floor with another department and I don't even recognize the people walking around. They're all new because all of the previous employees abandoned the company."

"Turnover is costly for employers. Keeping everyone happy is a never-ending problem. You have to maintain a healthy level of tolerance, but you should never be in a work situation that compromises your health or sanity. Don't settle for a work situation where you feel sick to your stomach all day, every day. If you experience these feelings on an ongoing basis, you need to find something else.

"Because you're in the early stages of your career, where you are may be a stepping stone. Regardless of how they treat you, you have your credentials. Before I became a business owner, the corporation I worked at didn't value training or mentoring. It was a tough environment to work in but I constantly reminded myself that I was a CPA with potential. I never let them distract me from my career goals."

"They seem to make it impossible to get to the next level."

"If you're not sure how to reach the next level, ask how that level is attained. Your employer needs you to carry out tasks; otherwise, she has to do them herself. Make yourself indispensable and ask valuable questions.

"Add some business books to your reading list. You can leverage knowledge from authors with many years of business experience and bring that to the table in your workplace. The best career advice I ever read suggested that you learn everything you possibly can about your employer. Even if you are in a department that seems distant from the rest of the company, you can learn about your employer's business. How does it earn income? What are its business segments? How does it market their products? What are its accounting policies? The more you know about your employer, the more valuable you become.

"What do the CEO and the CFO worry about? Are they considering acquisitions of small competitors? Are they considering selling parts of the company or the entire company? Have you read your employer's annual report? Is there any public information that you can retrieve that will help you understand your employer's business strategy? Are there published press releases? You'll have an opportunity to gain confidence and hold your own in any company meeting if you relate your role in the company to the overall objectives of your employer."

"No one ever tells us that. They sort of expect us to "get it," even though they offer no support," Ally said.

"Most people are busy holding their head above water. It's up to you to learn as much as you can on your own. Read business books. You can never read too many."

"How do I ensure that I'm on the right path?"

"Use the annual evaluation process of your employer to assess your skill development. What are your greatest strengths and weaknesses? Where are your shortcomings? List them. You want to know what areas need improvement and be honest with yourself.

"You can also ask questions. Your employer owes you answers to the following:

- What should I keep doing?
- What should I stop doing?
- How can I be more valuable?
- What alternate paths do you see me being successful in?

"If you have a specific area you are interested in, request to work in that group. Ask what type of training would be helpful before you make a switch.

"One critical skill to develop is learning how to communicate. Improve on your writing skills as well as your verbal skills. Practice writing complaint letters whether or not you send them. Practice writing opinion letters to a newspaper or magazine editor. Write in good sequence, re-read your work with a critical eye, and make corrections. Ask someone to read your work and give honest feedback. Make sure that your writing is clear and understandable. Ask your audience a question that helps you know if your point has been conveyed in the manner you intended. Rephrase anything ambiguous or confusing. Look at one sentence and practice rephrasing it into two sentences. This will help you express your point of view. Expand on your point by giving rich descriptions. Fully support your point of view."

Ally agreed that communication skills were an asset and an area she could work on. "Writing is a very difficult process but I'm starting to recognize that when I read someone else's poor writing, I don't want my work to represent me in that light," she said.

"It's important to recognize others' weaknesses and learn from them," Victoria told her. "Be very careful of everything you put your name on. You never know whose hands it will end up in. Practice writing about your career projects. Write out your projects as if you need to explain them to someone completely unrelated to your field. Good communication is about knowing your audience. Your audience is relying on you to fully explain the details of your material. Pretend they have no knowledge of your subject and need you to break it down into small nuggets of information. It is your responsibility to tie those bits of information together. Making sure you are fully understood starts with your ability to express yourself in full. You can start out with the smallest projects to practice."

"Can you give me some examples? I'm not sure how to get this off the ground."

"I had a supervisor who kept sending a document back to me. His criticism was harsh even though he offered no suggestions. I realized I had to take control of this situation. I went to a bookstore after work and bought a book on business writing. It was geared toward technical engineering which was outside my field. Nonetheless, the message was the same. Writing has to be clear and organized, with sufficient support for the ideas being expressed. I took the book to work the following day and revised my document using the suggested methods. I'm also diligent about using a thesaurus. After I submitted the revision, my never-easy-to-please supervisor did something he never did before. He complimented my work. You have the ability to turn situations around in the same way."

"That's an encouraging story." Ally realized that she too was capable of turning situations in her favor, if she handled them the right way.

"Don't forget to improve your verbal communication skills as well. You'll be expected to express yourself in an intelligent manner. Unfortunately, your superiors won't teach you this. Take a class in learning verbal skills such as Dale Carnegie, or join a Toastmasters group. You'll be guided toward speaking more confidently. This training will be invaluable in your career. Your superiors will not promote you or give you positions that require visibility if you can't portray yourself assertively and confidently. Spend time learning to write clearly and then practice a verbal presentation of your writing. Practice speaking with confidence, not hesitation.

"Let me give you some other workplace habits to avoid. Don't ever delegate up."

"What do you mean?"

"That means telling your manager what her job is or trying to pawn your work off on your manager."

"I would never do that, but I work with some people who have done that."

"Don't associate with people who try that manipulation. It makes you look bad if you keep those people in your company and will diminish the perception of your skill set in your manager's eyes.

"Don't constantly complain. Come up with solutions. Anyone can place blame and gripe, but it takes a thinking person to come up with solutions. Always try to offer a solution if something is not working.

"Never intentionally make your immediate manager look bad. Your manager wants you to make her life easier. Don't complain about a manager taking the credit for everything that you do. Some managers do that, but you can always make sure that you get credit for your work by keeping a running list of your projects and accomplishments. Make sure to submit a self-assessment at evaluation time. No one can deny your value if you produce a detailed list with examples of your work.

"One thing that cannot be reversed is when you have gone over your manager's head to complain. No one appreciates that and when you become a manager, you won't either. Work out your issues with the person first before speaking to anyone else. Express your discontent in a calm, professional manner. Again, offer solutions to make the situation better. Ask what you can do, then do it. There is no better way to gain credibility than to follow through on your promises.

"Leave your emotional baggage home. Don't whine about your personal problems. You may, of course, get to know people and they will get to know you, but you want to keep certain aspects of your life private."

"What's the harm in talking about your personal life?"

"It may seem like fun if you are talking about something crazy that you did or some silly situation you are in, but there are people who may make that the subject of the next office joke. You can be personal, but keep it light. Avoid being unprofessional and immature."

"What if you work for someone who doesn't appreciate you? My manager is OK but I have friends who hate their managers."

"If you are working for someone who doesn't support you or is constantly critical, it is time to consider working elsewhere. Don't waste valuable time working for someone who doesn't support your development. You won't make the necessary advances in your skill set if you work in a dead-end position.

"There are bad managers everywhere and sometimes it seems that the least-appropriate people get the manager positions. Some have no social skills at all and irritate their subordinates all day long. It's unfortunate, but it happens."

"Some places are so small that it's hard to advance," Ally added.

"That's also true. It can be the best place to work but if there is no room for advancement, then it's time to move on to something more challenging. People become complacent and sacrifice their earnings potential by staying in the same place for too long without advancement. This can take years to overcome. After a while, a person's marketable skills will be on the decline. When that person decides to move on, she won't be competitive with other candidates."

"How do I make sure that that doesn't happen to me?"

"Use your best judgment. If you can find a mentor at your job, that would be ideal. If there are no mentors to approach, make sure that you are on a good track and are being appropriately supported. Everyone has to wait for promotions, but if you are being strung along for more than two years, it's time to start looking. Keep the pulse on your career and manage it.

"As a crossover to your finances, keep in mind that your employer is helping you save for retirement as well. Don't take that for granted. I see that one of your goals is to fund your employer retirement plan. I can't overemphasize this issue. Make sure you are taking full advantage of your employer benefits. Max out your employer match. If your employer will match your retirement contribution up to three percent, make sure that you are electing the three percent contribution. When leaving an employer don't make the disastrous common mistake of withdrawing the retirement account balance without rolling it over. Even if it's a small amount of money, every little bit counts. The accumulation of small amounts over a very long period of time is what makes 401(k) account holders millionaires. Choose the accounts carefully. Read the information for the choices and be cognizant of the account fees. When you get a raise, be sure to increase your contribution percentage. Trust me; you will not even miss the money.

"Another thing to do is plan your benefit usage carefully. For example, if you've had a visit at the eye doctor, skip a year before the next appointment. Sometimes the eye doctor will tell you not to come back for two years. When you buy a new pair of glasses and can get two years out of them, you can skip paying for your vision benefit for a year. It may not sound like much, but in that year that's one less payroll deduction."

"Even if you do participate in an employer-sponsored retirement plan, you can still make contributions to an Individual Retirement Plan or a Roth IRA."

"I can?"

"Absolutely. You need to stay under the minimum income requirements to make a Roth IRA contribution, but you can contribute up to the maximum each year."

MAKING PEACE WITH THE PAST

The annual family vacation, taken in July, was at a resort in the Catskills in upstate New York. Ally had many wonderful childhood memories of the family vacations spent in the bucolic setting, and she was looking forward to the week.

Ally's brother picked her up on a Friday to set off on a week of water sports, hiking, and barbeques. This year would be special because it was going to be a family reunion of aunts, uncles, and cousins from outside New York. It was her parents' thirtieth anniversary and they had invited everyone from the family to join them.

Ally spent time with cousins that she had lost touch with, and caught up with her brother and parents. When the group settled in for the evening, Gail pulled Ally aside to ask about Ally's meetings with Victoria.

"So, you said you would tell me all about what you've been discussing with Victoria."

"I'm learning so much from her, Mom. There are so many aspects to money management that I never knew about."

"I hope you don't feel like Dad and I shortchanged you in any way," Gail said.

"Of course not. I've learned that every generation has its own way of dealing with finances and you offered what you knew from your experiences. I've also realized that no matter what impression of money management I learned in the past, it can be adjusted to help me create my own habits for self-sustenance."

"What specific things have you learned?" Gail asked, finding herself more curious than jealous.

"Victoria has helped me to understand that society sometimes teaches us certain things about money defined by social roles. But those social roles may not serve an adequate purpose. I was uncomfortable with my finances and because I want to do things on my own, and not rely on a husband, I needed to make a change. She's helped me create a roadmap for change. It starts with paying off my debt, then learning how to spend carefully."

"I always told you not to overspend," Gail responded.

"I know, Mom. It's a little more than that. She's given great career advice and taught me about basic financial topics like how to determine your personal net worth, balance sheets, and cash flow analysis."

"She always was money-smart. I knew that from the time we first met."

"She gives these great little speeches on the weekends to groups of women to help them as well. You should come, Mom."

"Maybe I will. I'm really glad you're learning all this, even if you didn't get it from me. You don't understand the fears of having to provide for a family, and how that affected the decisions we made. We did the best we could. The world is so different now and there are things that Dad and I wouldn't be able to give you advice on. Women didn't have the opportunities that you have now."

"I understand, Mom, and you don't have to explain."

Ally and Gail both felt relieved to have aired their feelings. Ally didn't want her mom to feel at fault. Likewise, Gail didn't want Ally to feel that she had been an inadequate role model.

HOUSEHOLD SPENDING

The time that Ally invested in reading about financial topics was paying off; she was feeling more intelligent in these discussions. Whether it was asking the right questions or recognizing things that she didn't focus on before, she was growing in ways she never expected.

"How's your spending working out?" Victoria asked.

"I was reading about spending for household investments. Can we talk about that?"

"Of course. Household investments can be thought of in terms of nonfinancial and financial. Nonfinancial assets are household assets that are used in everyday living, like a washing machine and dryer. These tangible items are called real assets. These include the home, furniture, kitchen appliances, and personal-use car. Other nonfinancial assets include income-earning qualities, physical skill sets, anticipated inheritances, and other situations related to personal scenarios that are intangible but provide the ability to earn income. Additional nonfinancial assets are items of worth such as jewelry and collectibles. Financial investments are the typical stocks, bonds, and mutual funds.

"The manager of the household makes decisions by determining which assets will benefit the household in the preferred time period. In a simple example, you would decide to purchase a coffee maker and make your own coffee at home instead of buying it every morning. This would benefit you in two ways—by saving time and by saving the cost. How quickly would the coffee machine pay for itself?

"Another example would be to buy a washing machine to wash clothes at home instead of having to spend time and money at the laundromat.

"A more complicated example would be whether to stay at a current job, anticipating future raises, or going back to school to create a different career. The potential income of the two career paths would be analyzed and the option with the higher return on human assets would be chosen. Either way, the individual would be spending time building a career, but may choose the option that provides the highest return on the human time investment.

"Purchasing a home or renting is a critical decision that would be analyzed the same way."

"Is it better to rent or buy?"

"To fully analyze these purchases, you could apply capital budgeting techniques such as net present value or internal rate of return calculations. But it doesn't have to be that complicated. Everyone needs a place to live, right? How would you measure renting a home or buying, in a practical sense? Houses and land tend to appreciate in value; that's not a consideration when renting a house or apartment. However, houses must be maintained and in good repair. Home improvements must be considered in a lifetime budget. The advantages of home ownership play a part in the decision. Privacy, security, and wealth building add to the attraction of making a home purchase. The home provides multiyear benefits."

"I think I would rather buy and have the security of a place to call my own."

"Don't buy unless you plan to stay for several years."

"I've read that's the most important consideration. Why is that?"

"Real estate is not a liquid asset. You can't unload it easily. If you have to move for your job or if you had reservations about the area you chose, it may not be that easy to sell. If the value temporarily goes down, you may be stuck. As an example of the worst case, many people bought when real estate prices were inflated and now their home is worth less than their mortgage value."

Ally sat back and tried to see into the future. "I think I'll just save up for a while and make my decision when it suits my lifestyle better."

LEARNING FROM YOUR FRIENDS' MISTAKES

Ally met Amy for lunch in the company cafeteria. Ally had been preoccupied with learning financial concepts and she didn't want to bore everyone around her with constant money topics. But what Taylor had recently done was something Ally would never consider. After they talked about Amy's upcoming wedding plans, Ally couldn't hold it in anymore.

"I can't believe what my friend Taylor did."

"What happened?"

"She called me to tell me that she is starting a new job next week."

"OK, what's wrong with that?"

"She then also told me she bought a new SUV."

"OK, still not so bad." Amy was confused.

"Well, she withdrew all the money from her 401(k) when she resigned from the old job, and used the money to buy the SUV. She took out the entire fifteen thousand and still has a car loan to boot."

"Oh, not good."

"No kidding. I asked her why she did that. She just blew it off, like, Oh, I have the rest of my life to work and I needed a new car. I reminded her that she takes the train to work and will be driving the SUV to the train station."

"That's not smart."

"No, from what I've been reading, the opportunity to benefit from compounded returns over three decades would have made that fifteen thousand dollar account worth close to one million dollars, even at a conservative rate of three percent annually."

"That's an example of What-Not-To-Do."

"Not only did she empty that starter retirement account, but it seems that she's spending her extra paycheck income on the car payment. The fifteen thousand didn't cover the entire cost of the SUV and the monthly insurance payment is ridiculous. You know, I grew up with Taylor but I don't think I can stay close with her anymore. We don't gel on the same level."

"I know. I have friends that I've grown apart from. They either got married years before me or we just didn't have anything in common anymore. Don't agonize over it. You're not alone."

"You're right. I guess it's time to move on. One takeaway is that it's good to learn from others' mistakes. I know I'll never be emptying my 401(k) when I leave a job. That's like committing the ultimate financial sin."

"You won't be leaving here. You'd miss me too much!"

CREDIT SCORE FIXES

Based on Victoria's suggestions, Ally started to think about how to increase her credit score. When Ally checked, her FICO score was six hundred ten. Her goal was to get it above seven hundred fifty, and it wasn't too far to go. It wasn't too late for damage control.

Ally had just received a new credit card offer to transfer balances and pay zero percent interest for six months. If she transferred her big balances to that account, she would at least be relieved of the interest charges. Then, she could get the secured credit card account and use it only for necessary purchases. Ally knew she'd have to make a deposit to obtain the secured line of credit, but she'd have about three hundred dollars in two months and could get by until then. The balance for any necessary purchases would be paid in full each month, in addition to reducing the large balance.

Ally picked up one of the books she had checked out from the library. She wanted to learn a little bit more about what goes into a credit score. There were five major categories.

1. Payment history: This accounts for thirty-five percent of the score.

2. Amounts currently owed: Thirty percent of the score is based on this. This includes not only credit card balances but also home loans and car loans. The credit card balances can do the most damage here. Obviously it's good to try to keep the credit card balances as low as possible.

3. Length of credit history: This makes up about fifteen percent of the total score. The longer the history, the better. Good payment history accounts should not be closed.

4. Types of credit: This accounts for about ten percent. There should be a healthy mix of accounts (i.e., not all credit card accounts). Credit card, home loan, and car loans should be balanced.

5. Searches for new credit: This also accounts for about ten percent. This category reflects how often a person is seeking credit. It shouldn't be frequent; that's a bad sign.

Keeping all this in mind allowed Ally to have a better focus on how she was managing her accounts and balances.

Mini-goals:

Transfer balances to zero percent account

Open up secured credit card account

Set up calendar reminders in phone to make payments

Set up calendar reminder to re-check score in six months

PLAYING MIND GAMES

Victoria didn't have a formal script in mind for today's presentation. She scanned the crowd to sense the vibe. She noted how several of the young women carried the latest handbag. Almost all had highlighted hair. Salon highlights were expensive. Victoria wondered how they could afford it? And, why would they spend money to excess? Hair highlights weren't a necessity; neither was a fancy handbag. Now she had an idea.

Let's talk about how not to spend money, and feel good about it. What are the best ways to not spend money? Let's play some mind games.

I like to go to the mall, browse, and then buy nothing. I might make some mental notes about things that I will save for, but I will not buy anything on the spot.

You can psyche yourself out in so many ways to enhance savings. To make it not hurt so much, use the envelope, jar, or bucket approach. This works very effectively, builds on small amounts very quickly, and is painless. This also works by setting up different bank accounts for different purposes and making regular deposits to each. Better yet, set up automatic checkbook deductions. Then there will no wavering from the plan. This method requires some discipline and you need to be careful not to go into overdraft with other monthly expenses.

Some people increase their tax withholding as a means of saving. Then when their tax refund comes back, they save the entire amount. That's not the most efficient money management, but it works for some.

The next time you get a raise, take the paycheck increase and save that portion. You lived without it before, right? Also, automatically increase your 401(k) election amount when you get a raise. You will not even notice the difference. The compounding returns of that small amount will exponentially increase for the duration of your working years.

You can reduce the opportunity for impulse spending by depositing money into the types of accounts that make it difficult to withdraw easily, such as IRAs, annuities, and life insurance policies.

Save up cash in advance, think before making purchases, and decide how long you can do without something before taking the leap. Overall, be honest with yourself. Do you really need another pair of shoes or pants? Can you eliminate extras by taking action on your own? Too many "added" services provide conveniences but can add to any bill.

Learn how to make small repairs, learn to sew buttons. I know someone who paid fifty dollars for buttons to be re-sewn onto her coat. A simple sewing kit costs way less than that and they are sold everywhere. That is clearly a waste of money! I knew a young man who would throw shirts away if they were missing a button. Really! Listen up and learn how to thread a needle.

As far as small repairs, necessity is the mother of invention —and learning. My former coworker suffered significant pay cuts after 2008. While he would have normally replaced his water heater when it began leaking—at a cost of eight hundred dollars—he looked into making the repair himself because he didn't have eight hundred dollars. It cost him less than ten dollars to buy the faucet part that attached to the water heater. He shut the valve, removed the broken faucet, and replaced it with the new part. He saved seven hundred ninety dollars by learning how to make a simple repair on his own.

Practice living cheap. It's fun to pay as little as possible. It feels good to get by without having to constantly be spending money. You might be thinking that it also feels good when you bring everything home, right? But what about that bill hangover? That bill is on its way from the second you walk out of the store. If you haven't saved up in advance . . . ouch!

Practice paying as little as possible for your needs. Make it a treasure hunt. Search craigslist, eBay, and Amazon for what you need. Have patience, specify what you want, and make sure you let others know what you need. When they need to sell it, they will seek you out.

I once bought a piece of exercise equipment that retails for four hundred fifty dollars and paid one hundred fifty. Better than that, the seller delivered it to my house, free of charge. She had needed to downsize to a smaller apartment and the equipment was in her storage unit. She needed the hundred and fifty dollars. I made sure to buy it from someone in my area so that it was convenient for me and the seller. I have a coworker who paid five dollars for several sets of weights from a garage sale. The homeowner said his son had bought all the weights and never used them.

This can equate to saving thousands, especially when it comes to real estate. Vacation timeshares can be bought for a fraction of their full price when purchased from an existing owner.

See? Anything can be bought at an affordable price. Buy things used. Go to the library. Trade things with friends.

Mock the world for a little while. Refuse to spend more than you need to . . . for anything. Visit thrift shops and see how little you can spend on something fabulous. Many thrift shops are designer only.Check out Rent the Runway. For thirty dollars you can rent a cute little number for a night out or an event.

Don't ever tell yourself stories to rationalize a large-dollar purchase. We are all good at convincing ourselves that we've made a good purchase, even if we had to go into debt to do it. Start telling yourself different stories. The typical law-of-attraction wish is to draw in millions of dollars and have big wealth. Turn that on its head by declaring that you will acquire everything you want, but at the cheapest price under the sun. You will have what you desire but will not have laid out big dollars for it.

AMY AND DAVID

Amy and David had not talked to each other all day. Amy was furious with David, and she spewed out her anger with Ally.

"How dare he spend two hundred dollars on a football jersey when we're trying to save money for our wedding? He didn't even ask me. I found out from my brother."

Ally nodded, shaking her head. "I know, I know… I'm working on a financial plan, like we talked about. Your situation has me worried about choosing a man to marry," she told her coworker.

"But we just talked the other night about how we want to work toward our goals and be careful with what we spend. We also talked about which band we wanted for our wedding and how much everything is costing us. He brought up how I spent a ridiculous amount on my dress, but at least that was for the wedding."

Amy and David became engaged four months ago. Amy just turned twenty-eight and has known David for three years. She knows he has some bad spending habits. He's a bit on the immature side but she was working on communicating her plans to him—and hoping he was getting the hint.

It wasn't going exactly as she planned. Case in point: the expensive football jersey.

"You two really need to get on the same page," Ally said. She didn't want to be too forward with advice; sometimes people are offended.

"How do I do that? I can't be with him every minute," Amy complained.

My financial confidante says it's important to come up with a plan, but nothing too painful to start with."

"What exactly do you do on this plan?"

"Where you lay out all your monthly income, pay your must-pay debts, and then pay yourself first to build a savings balance. Then what you have left over will be your spending money."

"How do I convert David?"

"Maybe you can keep separate accounts and have him transfer over to you whatever you decide on. Then you can't say he hasn't put up his share."

"But we wanted to pool everything together."

"Sometimes you can't do that, especially if one half of the couple doesn't prioritize and makes frivolous buys."

"That's a good idea. David and I will have to have a serious talk about this."

"It's similar to opening a separate bank account to make regular deposits into."

"Maybe we should just open a separate account—without an ATM card. That way, there won't be any temptations to make withdrawals."

"That's a better idea. You could both make regular deposits into it and use it toward a goal, like a house, or right now, for your wedding arrangements."

"That's a great idea! Thanks," Amy looked a little less stressed and was glad she had talked to Ally about her fiancé's spending.

"Let me know what happens."

"I will. Thanks!"

Ally was shocked at her own realization of how easy it was to find solutions to savings dilemmas. It all stemmed from her get-togethers with Victoria. The more she talked about her money situation, the more she thought of money-saving ideas. It was as simple as creating awareness and exercising the habits. By being cognizant of spending habits, she was able to cut corners here, there, and everywhere. She realized she could exercise some patience with her spending. By waiting for the next credit card cycle, she delayed the charge for a month. All the little things really added up.

Ally had saved one thousand dollars after four months and was thrilled when she checked her bank balance. It was hard, but so worth it now. It wasn't a ton of money, but it gave her some breathing room.

She couldn't wait to tell Victoria. She also couldn't wait to tell her that she had paid down her credit card balance by twelve hundred dollars as well. More importantly, the only additional charges were necessities that were well thought out in advance.

RETIREMENT DILEMMA

Victoria went to the local ladies club for a lunch session. The club's members were a cross-section of local volunteers, professionals, and women from various community organizations. She noticed her friend Catherine getting a cup of coffee. She and Catherine had not seen each other in several months so Victoria made her way across the room to say hello.

"Hello, Catherine. How have you been?"

Catherine was a bit startled, but relaxed after looking up and seeing Victoria. "Hello, Victoria! So nice to see you. You look great!"

"Thank you. Glad to see you here." Victoria wanted to return the compliment but noticed that Catherine looked stressed. "Is everything OK? Let's sit down and catch up." Victoria poured herself herbal tea and walked to a nearby open table.

They sat down and Catherine updated her on her job, her grandchildren, and her husband's latest health issues.

Victoria remembered that Catherine was nearing age sixty, almost eligible to collect Social Security. Her husband had a great career as a corporate executive. Catherine only worked part time for many years and was quick to constantly remind others that she didn't need to work full time. Victoria didn't usually tolerate uppity attitudes but stayed on friendly terms with Catherine in spite of the attitude that she dished out to others.

Based on her demeanor, it seemed as if her circumstances had changed since those years of bragging.

"Jim is not well these days. He has precancerous tumors in his throat. The surgery is dangerous but there are some options. Unfortunately, he doesn't feel well on most days so we have to take immediate steps."

"Oh, I'm so sorry to hear that."

"He is struggling at home by himself, and with my children gone, I can only do what I can when I'm not working."

"You only work part time; can't you retire?"

"I really can't retire until I'm eligible for Social Security benefits. We need the money right now. Jim's Social Security income can't cover all of our household expenses, so I guess I have to continue working until then. It's not much, but it's something and it helps.

"I'm two years from reaching age sixty-two but even then, my monthly amount will be reduced. I really can't afford to start collecting at age sixty-two. I would like to wait until I'm at least sixty-seven, but that won't be an option now. I may have to take a leave of absence, without pay, and then return when I'm able to. That's if they hold my job. Part-timers don't have much leverage."

Victoria sat back and listened sympathetically.

"My Social Security amount is not that much because I only worked part time for the last twenty years. I guess I never thought that we would have financial issues."

"Does Jim have a pension?" Victoria asked.

"Yes, but only for the years before the pension benefit was terminated. His company stopped funding that plan fifteen years ago. So, it's a little bit, not a huge monthly sum."

Victoria felt terrible for Catherine. What a dilemma to have at the end of all of their working years. This should be a time to enjoy life, now that her husband's years of working hard were over. Victoria thought about adding this to her discussions with Ally. Surely, a young professional would not think that far ahead, but it was worth mentioning.

There are so many factors to consider and the decisions change as people progress through their lives. Some people may work part time for a period of their lives but once things change, it's critical to engage in full-time employment to have full benefits in addition to a paycheck.

Shortsightedness and time elapsed usually only allows for limited choices in the end. Another unfortunate situation is spending all your retirement years going to doctor appointments. Imagine working hard your whole life to end up in poor health. Victoria wrote herself a reminder to emphasize this issue with Ally in the future. One of the keys of an adequate financial plan is anticipating medical issues that can't be avoided.

INVESTING

After six months, Ally realized that she had reduced her credit card principal by almost two thousand dollars and she had saved sixteen hundred dollars. It was a great feeling. It was also good knowing that she hadn't made any frivolous purchases in the past six months.

The cold weather was setting in and with it, the seasonal depression. The constant discipline felt stark and austere. Month after month, the doldrums of self-restraint made life a little boring.

It's going to be a tough winter.

Ally hit the Pause button. *This is where I walk the walk, and talk the talk. This is where the strong survive and go the distance. It's so much easier to give in and get some retail therapy, but I know the un-retail method is how it's done and there's no way around it.*

Ally knew that a healthy bank balance was not just going to show up one day. It had to be earned and built up. Money had never fallen out of the sky and it wasn't starting now. Saving today meant having more tomorrow. That was the bottom line.

Ally needed to find out what she was made of. And she was going to prove to herself that she could stay the course. She immediately logged into her bank account and stared at her savings balance. That would serve as a reminder of her progress. She looked at the history of transfers into the account, which were so methodical. She wanted to keep the pattern going.

With the seasons changing, she would need a good pair of boots to get through the sloppy weather but would wait for a sale. She also needed a new coat, but would layer up for now and then buy one after New Year's when they all go on sale.

Ally adopted three new mini-goals:

1) Examine spending journal and eliminate one expense

2) Try to double savings

3) Pick one regularly purchased item and only buy it at a reduced price

It was time to think about investing. This was one of her original goals but she knew it would be addressed after the move to a new apartment and initially learning how to start managing how she spent her money.

Well, now was the time. This would be her main topic when talking with Victoria.

There are so many things to invest in and it was so confusing. *Do I choose mutual funds or stocks? What are an ETF and a Spider?* Ally knew investing was important but wasn't sure exactly why.

"I've been thinking about investing, Victoria. Can you help me to understand what I need to do?"

"So glad you asked. It's very important to invest. Remember, you're only one person and can only do the work of one person. But if you invest and earn from the work of others, you'll have leveraged the use of your money to benefit from the work of many. There are different ways that smart investing helps you earn off the backs of others' efforts. It can be done by investing into a business that has many workers or by buying stocks that pay dividends. If you understand that your earnings can be translated into building an empire for yourself, you will find the opportunities. That way, your earnings grow for you and your wealth will increase exponentially. You don't want to stay only invested in cash. You'll miss growth opportunities. To sum it up, the premise of investing is in alignment with having your money work for you."

"What factors should be considered?"

"You want to consider your investment timeline. You wouldn't invest in long-term, illiquid securities if you planned on needing the money soon. For example, it wouldn't be wise for people to invest in a five-year Certificate of Deposit (CD) if they know they'll be paying for their child's college education within one year. They would pay a penalty for early withdrawal, reducing the funds. Instead, they would be better off investing in a one-year CD or something that they could easily and quickly convert into cash when they needed it, like a stock index fund or bond fund."

"OK, I'll keep that in mind when I'm thinking about buying a house."

"Now you need to think about if you want to actively invest or passively invest. I would suggest that you passively invest as you'll need to focus on your career. You need to put time into research to become a wealthy active investor. Unless you can invest your time and services in the business that you're investing in, you should be cautious and invest passively.

"Think of your investments in conjunction with your other assets as part of your total portfolio. This is similar to an asset allocation approach and would include a house, a car and any other possessions accumulated along the way. Don't forget to include your human asset as well, that is, your ability to work and earn income."

"So, it's an overall approach?"

"Absolutely."

"What's the difference between a stock and a bond?"

"When you buy a stock, you're an equity owner. As a bond owner, you're lending money to the company."

"So, it's two different ways of ownership?" Ally asked.

"They're two different financial instruments. As a shareholder, you own a fraction of the company and are entitled to a share of the company's profits. A bondholder's ownership terminates when the bond issuance is satisfied. I'll explain.

"As I said, when you own a share of stock, you own a portion of the company. You should consider your ownership as significant as that of the largest shareholder because, relatively speaking, it's just as important. You only own a smaller dollar amount but are nonetheless an owner.

"A bond ownership starts when the company issues a specific bond. I'll use a simple example. A company needs one million dollars to purchase equipment. They issue a bond to investors over a period of five years with the agreement to pay three percent interest in exchange for the use of the money. By the way, that's what interest is. It's a payment in exchange for the use of someone else's money."

"How are the bonds sold? Does one person lend the entire one million dollars?"

"Great question. Typically, bonds are sold in smaller denominations. For purposes of this example, let's say they sell the bonds in one thousand dollar denominations."

"So, what happens during the duration of the bondholder's ownership?"

"The bondholder receives interest payments at specified times, such as semi-annually or annually. At the end of the five years, the bondholder gets the principal amount back."

"The principal amount is the amount of the initial loan, right?"

"Exactly, and the end of the loan period is called the maturity date. I don't want to get too complicated but it's ideal to have a mix of both bonds and stocks. So, getting back to stocks, you need to know a few things before investing. When you research a publicly traded company to invest in, there are a number of things to look for. First of all, you will need to read the company's annual report. You want to determine the credibility of management and see stability in their business venture. Annual reports are available to the public and can be obtained with a simple Internet search. When you delve a little deeper, you will want to get some background on the top executives and see what their track record is like. Such as, are they newcomers? Do they have a background in the industry?"

"Where are the annual reports on the company's website?"

"They're usually found when you click on the Investor Relations link. As you continue, you will want to look for the company's key statistics such as a history of earnings per share and debt ratios. Other financial ratios are helpful as well, but let's stay with the basics for now. You can always research what you don't know."

"Are there different ways of purchasing stocks?"

"Stocks can be purchased individually or in a mutual fund. Mutual funds are pooled stock or bond accounts. Your investment money is pooled with other investors and the portfolio manager makes decisions on the investments in the portfolio. It's best to understand the portfolio manager's investment strategy. Find out how long the portfolio manager has been with the fund. Do some research on the individual and see what you can find out about his or her history. You are trusting this person with your hard-earned money."

"Are mutual funds all the same?"

"Mutual funds are as different as the individuals managing them. They can be specific to a certain industry or sector of the economy, like technology or energy. They can represent US or foreign companies or focus on a specific market capitalization threshold. There are an abundance of mutual funds to choose from. You should try to narrow down your choices first before doing Internet research or the decision will be overwhelming. Money market funds are another type of mutual fund. This type of fund typically is very low-risk and invests in short-term securities issued by corporations and US and state governments."

"What else should I consider?"

"Develop a strategic approach to asset allocation and consider the long term."

"What do you recommend for choosing stocks?"

"Here are some ideas. You can start with a stock index fund. An index fund mimics the movement of a stock index. The fund owns the same stocks that are in the index. No matter what you invest in, always be careful of the costs of the investment, including the costs of obtaining an investment manager.

"Another way of investing is value investing. Value investing means that you are buying company stocks that are slightly undervalued. That way, you have the best opportunity to have growth. You wouldn't buy an overvalued stock, the same as not buying an overvalued house.

"Do the research on value investing. You have the luxury of having the Internet to help you. Decades ago, one had to go to the library and hope that the collection had enough choices to address the specific questions. The Internet is practically real time and there are tons of resources to go to. You should use library books to supplement your Internet research.

"Save and invest. Don't invest foolishly; research and learn value investing. Think long term and don't make hasty decisions.

"You need to make your money work for you. Look at income-producing investments, where you can take that income and invest it again. Value investing is based on solid principles of companies that have a good track record, no debt, and use their capital wisely. Learn how to use an Internet stock screener. Google and Yahoo both have one."

"What's a stock screener?"

"The stock screeners allow you to enter in different variables and will perform a search on the companies that meet those definitions. For example, you can perform a search on technology companies that have a market capitalization of more than five hundred million. The search will return companies that meet that criteria. It's fun to play with."

"If I don't have much to start with, what are my options?"

"Another idea is dollar-cost average investing. This is also known as the constant-dollar plan, and it's easier to remember it that way. Dollar-cost averaging is a strategy that involves systematically investing a fixed amount of money instead of a lump sum. Investments are purchased when they are high and when they are low. That's how I started years ago. You can start with very small amounts. I still have some of the issued stock certificates. Now everything is electronic.

"This is a good way to introduce another concept: investing in DRIPs. DRIPs are dividend reinvestment plans. When you invest in a DRIP plan, you initially purchase shares that earn dividends. When the dividends are paid, the plan buys fractional shares of the same company's stock. Find a company that has a DRIP and start investing. Again, search the Internet. Over one thousand companies have a DRIP plan. Make purchases on a regular basis and let the dividends buy additional shares for you in your account. The minimum amount of each voluntary contribution to your account is typically fifty dollars. The investment allows you to buy fractional shares and the quarterly dividends will be reinvested. Companies that have DRIPs typically charge low or no fees.

"Always make sure your money is working for you. Whether it's to earn interest or dividends, or grow in value, always make sure you put your money to good use. You should look at your money as employees that go to work for you. Each dollar is an employee that can be put to work."

"What are most common investment mistakes?"

"Never, ever invest your money in risky ventures or you'll be disappointed with the result. You work hard, so don't waste your money. Also, don't watch the stock prices every day."

Ally wanted to relay a story. "Someone once asked me if I was interest in growth or income. That was annoying at the time because I'm interested in both. How could I possibly decide why one was better than the other? I'm not a retired person looking to live off dividends. By the time I retire, I would want my investments to have increased from growth but I would also want to have had dividends from the investments to reinvest. That's in alignment with compounding concepts. I can use current dividends to build up my stock ownership."

"Yes, I see what you mean," Victoria said. "You basically need liquidity and a good risk balance. Deciding between growth and income is a bit of a silly question. You want to make sure that you have liquidity to cover any emergency expenses if you need the money on short notice. However, there is nothing wrong with keeping it invested in a stock or mutual fund while you don't have immediate needs.

"Another suggestion is to read the mutual fund's prospectus carefully. A prospectus is the fund's selling document and will tell you the fund's strategy, initial investment, and expenses. It also tells you what types of securities are in the portfolio. Make sure that the expenses of purchase and sales commissions are not too high and that the mutual fund management fee is low. Find out the procedures to liquidate your investment."

"Is a hedge fund a mutual fund?"

"Another great question. A hedge fund is a pooled investment for a combination of securities. However, a hedge fund is a private investment that offers entry into the fund only to wealthy investors. Hedge funds are not mutual funds. Funds of funds are also not mutual funds."

"How do you determine which stocks are undervalued?"

"Market prices of stock don't always represent the underlying value of the stock. The company's value is based on its earnings. Earnings are the pulse of every company's value. Without earnings, a company won't survive. Therefore, don't assume that the market price of a stock determines the value. There are several key ratios that will help you determine the underlying value."

"Oh no, ratios. I'm not good at math."

"You don't have to be a math wizard to understand a few key concepts. When you translate those concepts into how they relate to the money you're investing, you'll see how simple this is.

"Let's start with a few simple concepts. The price/earnings ratio represents the market price per share divided by the annual earnings per share. Annual earnings per share is the annual earnings divided by the number of shares issued to shareholders. This is an amount that should be low, not high. The result of the ratio is the amount that would be invested to match one dollar of earnings. For example, if the price per share is seventy cents and the annual earnings per share is sixty cents, you would divide seventy by sixty. The resulting one dollar and sixteen cents means that for every one dollar and sixteen cents spent per share, there will be one dollar of annual earnings. Therefore, the lower the result of the ratio, the less money per share required to produce annual earnings. Thus, the more value for your investment.

"All of the components of these calculations can be obtained in Yahoo Finance, MSN Money, or the company's annual report. Would you like to know more?"

"Yes. That didn't sound so bad. I'm sure I might spend a little time with that calculation, but it's certainly doable."

"OK, then let's move on to the price/book ratio. The price to book ratio is the market price per share divided by the book value per share. Book value is a balance sheet term and represents the total assets of the business less the business's liabilities. Book value per share is calculated by dividing the book value by the amount of shares issued to shareholders. The result is the denominator of the price/book ratio. The market price per share is divided by the book value per share. Again, this value should be low. For example, if the price per share is ten dollars and the book value per share is eighty cents per share, the ratio would result in a twelve-dollar-and-fifty-cents price/book. That means that for every twelve dollars and fifty cents invested, it generates one dollar in equity. You would want to spend the least amount per dollar of equity, right? Again, more value for your investment."

"Right. I wouldn't have that much to invest, initially, so getting more value for my investment would be important. How else is the worth of a company determined?"

"What we've gone over so far are two key numerical factors, but there are many other factors that should be considered in making sensible investments. Some old-school tenets involve researching the management of the company; it should have a good track record. You are judging the integrity of the leaders of the organization. You might determine this by confirming that they put the company before their own needs and are not paid outrageous compensation amounts.

"The company should be stable. Stability would be evident by an increasing earnings per share over a long period of time. You can find the earnings per share in Yahoo Finance or MSN Money.

"One additional ratio would be the debt-equity ratio. It's fairly explanatory. It's the debt amount divided by the book value or equity of the company. This amount should be low, the same way your own debt-to-asset ratio should be low. You don't want to invest in a company with a high level of debt, as there is the risk of the company having to declare bankruptcy by not having ready cash to pay obligations. Once the company starts defaulting, the stock value will drop and the company may not be in business long."

"What's considered a high level of debt?" Ally asked.

"The debt to asset ratio should be less than fifty percent. Obviously, the lower the better."

"That makes sense." Ally stopped to underline a note in her book.

"Does that explanation makes it sound less intimidating? I hope you have a better understanding now. Let's take a break and consider the progress you've made. Are you pleased with all you've learned over the past six months?"

"I definitely am; this is all so interesting. I love to hear about business operations. I am going to apply this information to advance my career as well as plan and meet my financial goals."

"Good. Always think of your career skills as a gift and work your career with enjoyment, not with reluctance. Change your attitude toward money. Money should be seen as a bridge to all the things that you want out of life. Use it as a tool to get where you want to be. Don't think of your money situation as a shortage, even if it feels that way for now and until you pay off your debts. From now on, you need to think of money as ever-flowing and available for those who take the right steps."

MAKING SACRIFICES

Ally's cell phone was buzzing. She was in the library and couldn't take the call. Looking at the screen, she saw it was Taylor. She hadn't called Taylor in a few weeks. The last communication was to text her that she couldn't go to Jennifer's party. Taylor was disappointed but Ally kept the responses short. When Ally was done in the library for the day, she walked out of the building and called Taylor.

"Hey, Taylor. What's up?"

"Where have you been? I haven't heard from you. Why don't you call me?"

"Sorry, been busy with work. What's going on?"

"I wanted to tell you that we're planning a weekend up in the mountains to ski."

"When?"

"End of this month. You're coming, right?"

"Don't know. How much is the room?"

"It'll come to about three hundred dollars each but it depends on how many of us go."

"I don't want to be with ten other people in the room. How much if there are two people per room?"

"It'll definitely be three hundred dollars each just for the room if you and I share."

"Hmmm, not sure. But I'll let you know."

"Why the hesitation? Can I count on you?"

"Let me check my finances and get back to you. I'm not sure I'll have enough left over after paying my credit card bill down and saving."

"Are you kidding me? This is going to be the best weekend and you're going to miss it to pay off a credit card bill? You're no fun anymore!"

"You know, Taylor, some of us have other things to think about than going on a drunken weekend escape. This kind of expense will throw my whole budget into the toilet. We went last year and there will be other trips to take."

Taylor huffed into the phone.

"I said I would let you know. Besides, the payment for the room is not going to be the entire cost. We have to pay for equipment rental, the ski lift, meals, and transportation, right?"

"The room includes the equipment rental. The rest is nothing."

"No, it's something and those extra costs add up. I also have a wedding to go to this month. Between the dress and the gift, I decided to forgo spending on unnecessary things for a while."

"Since when did you become a nun?"

"A few months ago. Listen, gotta go. I'll let you know."

"We have to give the deposit and make the reservation by next week."

"Don't wait for me to make a reservation."

"What? You're not going to make the reservation?"

"No, I'm not. Gotta go. I'll call you."

Ally was not going to offer to put the entire bill on her credit card as she had in the past, even though Taylor now took it for granted. She had done that too many times and then waited for her friends to pay her back. Some had to be chased down. She could skip the ski trip this time. There would be others. That should be next on the list, save for a vacation.

THE COMPANY YOU KEEP

Victoria had been explaining the basics of financial planning but knew she needed to talk about how life's situations can derail the best of intentions. She wanted to be sure to discuss how outside factors cause interruptions. Victoria began by mentioning how people of different financial backgrounds can have conflicting expectations of each other.

"So, tell me if this sounds familiar. You are going out for dinner and your friends choose the priciest restaurant. Not only that, they order the most expensive thing on the menu and expect to split the bill evenly. Have you ever been in a situation where you felt uncomfortable?"

"Funny you should mention … I was roped into paying for something that I wasn't planning on. Taylor told me that we were just going to a happy hour with some friends. They were all sitting down to dinner. We joined them and stayed the entire evening. I wound up buying an expensive dinner and having to split the bill with the rest of the group. They ordered a costly bottle of wine that really drove up the bill."

"I know sometimes you can get caught in an awkward situation. Try to make some discreet suggestions the next time you see that coming. Be picky about the company you keep. If your friends are reckless with their money, you will be put in more situations that cause additional spending. It's the same as if you hang around people who eat too much. If they are only going to snack bars and restaurants for get-togethers, you'll do the same and find yourself gaining weight."

What a great analogy. It's true. Some of my friends spend money like it'll never end and I always wind up spending more than I intend to.

"I have to make sure that I talk to my friends in advance and solidify plans so I'm not stuck spending money that I don't want to."

"Did you have any other unexpected or unusual needs this month?"

"I had to pay for my friend's wedding gift. It took a chunk out of my budget."

"I'm sure you will have other weddings in the next few years. Starting now, plan for that expense in advance so it will not eat into your budget next year."

"Then, to top it off, Taylor expected me to go on a weekend ski trip and put the cost on my credit card to make the reservation for everyone. I decided not to go."

"Good for you for sticking to your goals."

"You know, some of my friends are already planning their inheritances."

"That's a bit dangerous. What if circumstances change? Anything can happen before their parents pass on. Their parents can become ill and need their money for medical care. Another sibling can have an emergency that requires their parents' assistance, grandchildren are born, parents divorce and remarry. An infinite number of situations can occur that can rob them of their plan. That's really not a smart mentality."

"I know someone who thought he would inherit his parents' home. His mom wound up running up all kinds of debt from a gambling habit. Now, the house is re-mortgaged."

"See? As I've said, that's why you can never depend on others for your financial security."

RETIREMENT INVESTING

The next time Ally visited Victoria, she jumped right in with enthusiasm and her built-up confidence.

"Victoria, my employer had a retirement investment seminar. Two companies came in and both gave great presentations on how he could create retirement investment accounts with them and they would beat the stock market."

"Were these for actively managed funds or for self-managed funds?"

"Both, I think. They promised to offer investment advice for anyone who wanted it but it was optional. I don't really know what to do. There seems to be so much research involved in finding the right investments. I feel like I'm just learning some basic things right now."

"I agree with that. There are differing points of view on this topic. In the one regard, it is better to have your money actively managed if you can't manage it yourself. At least the money manager will be making suggestions for you. However, you don't know if those suggestions are in your best interest and some money managers don't make good decisions. There are so many high-flying mutual funds from the 1980s and 1990s that are now defunct. They had many good years and then awful years. Some of those funds folded and faded into obscurity. Many people lost chunks of their investment portfolio by having their money in those accounts."

"What happened to them?"

"Those money managers took risky bets and made investments that suffered losses. They can't predict stock prices with any more certainty than you or I can. They try to sell themselves as capable of beating the market, but beating the market, and timing the market, rarely works out for any individual investor including the big-time asset managers. The securities invested in to reach an unattainable benchmark become so risky that it defeats the purpose of providing solid returns.

"You should also carefully consider the investment adviser fees. Investment advice fees can chip away at your account balance."

"I haven't really given that much thought."

"That's what they're hoping for. A management asset fee should not be higher than one percent of assets. Ideally, it should be as low as possible.

"Are the fees disclosed?"

"They are, but you have to be very careful about questioning your asset manager and reading the fine print of what you invest in. The government recently performed a study on the conflict of interest that exists when asset managers charge advisement fees and various other fees for investing money on an individual's behalf."

"How do they get away with this?"

"Individuals are left to their own accord in making investment decisions and will hire a professional financial adviser. There has been an explosion of options in funds and securities that makes it confusing for people to decide where to invest their money. It was discovered that almost half of all IRA assets are managed by professional financial advisers. Often, the adviser will influence a client to invest in the funds that benefit the adviser's earning potential instead of what's in the client's best interest. The government has revealed that while these financial advisers propose to offer advice in the client's best interest, they are working in their own best interest by offering investments that they will earn the highest commissions on. These payments are in the form of revenue-sharing fees, sales payouts, and commissions.

"Investors have expressed confusion about the amounts and types of fees they are charged. This is because the adviser invests the client's money in funds where the security fund fees are taken from the earnings before they even appear on the statements. Then the investment advisers take their fee on top of that. In addition, asset management fees are charged annually, based on the value of the portfolio. This ensures a perpetual income stream for the mutual fund and the adviser. The buildup of these fees can be excessive and significant. Employees don't always fully understand the options in their own 401(k) accounts.

"The government's report demonstrated how a one percent fee erodes an investment account over a long period of time. The account balance can suffer a twenty-five percent loss over that period of time.

"Some actively managed funds execute a large number of transactions in an effort to time the market. The government study showed that investment advisers did not dissuade their clients from investing in these funds. Portfolio managers that did attempt to time the market to produce exceptional returns were not always successful. Financial advisers tended to steer clients away from passively managed accounts, where excessive trading was avoided.

"A tax preparer I knew had an altercation with a client's financial adviser. She was reporting capital loss transactions on the client's tax return. They were losses that the client couldn't use currently and resulted in a capital loss carryforward. The financial adviser had placed the trades under the guise of executing trades in the best interest of the client. However, managers of actively traded accounts often place trades to generate commissions and perpetuate their earning potential. When the tax preparer questioned the financial adviser's motives, he became belligerent. The client was an elderly woman who didn't know any better. Unfortunately, this type of abuse occurs most frequently in accounts owned by the elderly.

"So, in general, be aware that you could be paying double fees."

"How would I know that?"

"If you own a fund that has an expense fee ratio, then move it under the purview of an investment adviser, your investment adviser then takes his or her fee in addition to what you already paid to own that mutual fund. Most times, people will move existing accounts and roll them into one portfolio but they fail to realize that each fund charges its own fees whether owned directly or through the asset manager.

"What compounds the reduction in the account is if the fund does not perform well and suffers a downturn, then the investment adviser will liquidate a portion of the fund and take the proceeds as a fee."

"What's the best way to invest in mutual funds, then?"

"Find the lowest-fee mutual fund that you can. Do several searches before making a decision. Own it directly, not through an asset manager. Ideally, you can diversify among several low-fee funds such as US stocks, international stocks, small-cap stocks, etc. Don't forget to include a bond fund. The bond fund will offset the stock volatility.

"Do some research offered by your employer. Ask what your employer's fund is invested in and understand the fee structure and the amount of the fees.

"Unfortunately, workers can no longer rely on pensions to support their retirement years. My grandparents retired with their pensions. Government workers are offered pensions for their tenure but the average working American is not offered a pension. The only source of retirement security is in a 401(k) account, savings, and equity in a residence. It is more important than ever to safeguard your account in every way possible."

BUYING REAL ESTATE

Ally envisioned living in her own house or a condo. It was one of her ultimate goals and she often daydreamed of how she would decorate her private surroundings. She had questions for Victoria about becoming a homeowner.

"If I want to buy a house or condo, where do I start?"

"I'm glad to see that you're thinking long term. That's the purpose of a financial plan—to develop a clear goal and move in the direction of obtaining what gives you fulfillment. Do you want to live in a mansion, or would a three-bedroom home suffice? Are you happiest living in an apartment with no property maintenance? Take some time and think it through.

"People think they want to live in Beverly Hills or East Hampton, but with that big mansion comes big maintenance. Buying the home is only the beginning of the expenses that must be covered to maintain it. The property taxes on a sprawling estate can be astronomical, not to mention the utility bills. When I see big homes, I see high monthly overhead—and lots of cleaning. If you know you will have the monthly income to cover those kind of expenses, you will be the envy of your friends and family. But you don't want to be house poor.

"Just like the early lessons I learned in life from neighboring families, it's not smart to get in over your head. It can be emotionally devastating to move into a home that you can barely afford. As the struggles snowball, you will be dodging an eventual foreclosure and the loss of the home. How have you planned on making this purchase? You need to be able to have fifteen to twenty percent as a down payment. There will be closing costs and mortgage insurance. Also, make sure that you have cash flow and "cushion" for unexpected expenses. You will probably be at Home Depot every day for the first few days and then make some less frequent trips during the first month."

"How do I get a mortgage?"

"You need to speak to a bank or mortgage company that will help define what type of loan will suit you best. But be careful. There are loans that can strangle you if you're not informed of your payment schedule. Make sure that you won't be house poor."

"What do you mean by house poor? You've mentioned it twice now."

"House poor means that you can only pay for your mortgage, taxes, insurance and upkeep of the home. If you barely have enough left over for food, transportation, and other expenses, you will be house poor. A good measure is spending no more than thirty percent of your disposable income on your home costs."

"What are the differences between the types of mortgages?"

"Try to apply for a fixed mortgage and avoid adjustable interest-only loans. Be careful of any mortgage that has a low interest rate and a large balloon payment. Always look to buy a home with the plan that you will remain there for the long term. Otherwise, buying may not even be worth it for you."

"Why not?"

"Some people think that they're only going to stay for a short time, because they have a starter home. They may wind up staying much longer than they think. Life happens, expenses pile up, and soon, they can't afford to move.

"You are best to take a thirty-year fixed mortgage to start with. That is your best chance to get on good grounds with a payment history."

"What's an adjustable mortgage?"

"That's a mortgage that adjusts the payments as the interest rate changes. Typically, they start with an attractive rate and payment, but then the interest rate "adjusts" and dramatically increases. For people who were not really qualified to own a home to begin with, the adjusted payment was not an amount they could afford and was a quick path to bankruptcy. I bought my first home with an adjustable mortgage, but the difference between my situation and what you've heard about with the 2008 crisis is that my career was on an upward trajectory at the time. Many people who entered into the adjustable mortgages in the 2000s did not have the resources to handle the adjusted payments."

Note to self, no adjustable mortgages.

"Most importantly, don't ever think of your home as an ATM. If the value increases, great. You have increased your net worth. But don't take on additional debt in the form of a home equity loan to pay for other expenses, such as a car, a vacation, etc.

"The home equity line of credit is an added mortgage payment that could put your home ownership in jeopardy. Especially if the value of your home decreases.

"Your life circumstances can easily change. If you are making more money, you can apply more money against the principal and pay the mortgage off faster. But don't rope yourself into sizing down your loan because the interest rate is lower.

"Monthly mortgage payments are *mandatory*. Leave yourself room. Some months are easier than others. Don't fall short because then you will have a black mark on your payment history and catching up can be hard to do. Expenses easily snowball and become unmanageable when the following month's living expenses will be on you."

Ally had lunch with her coworker Amy about a month later. Ally had been swamped at work but finally caught a break and wanted to get out of the office. She and Amy met at 12:30PM and went to a place that wasn't too noisy so that they could talk.

"So, how is David doing?"

"We finally worked out the money issue. He agreed that we should start setting some goals. He didn't regret buying that football jersey but agreed that he would start putting money aside to help pay his credit card debt down."

"Does he have a lot of credit card debt?"

"Yes, and I don't want it to cause a rift between us. He needs to pay it down, and fast. He agreed to open a new account so we could pool our money and set it aside for savings."

"Did you come to an agreement about how much you would both deposit on a regular basis?"

"Yes. We agreed to at least one hundred dollars a month, but he's a little slow at keeping his end of the bargain."

"Did you talk about how he needs to pay off the credit card debt?"

"Yes, and that's what's holding him up. He's paying the credit card debt down. At least he's doing something."

"I think opening up the new account sets you both up in the right direction. Maybe you can make a list of goals to work toward. Everybody needs motivation. Make a list of the things that you want to work toward. Start with the small things."

"That's a good thought. We could both keep to the list."

"It's helped me plan spending and avoid impulse buys. It makes you notice how you think about what you need versus what you want. It's easier to delay gratification because you know you'll have what you want—but not today. You'd be surprised how quickly you check things off the list. Eventually, you have what you want and need without being overextended."

That explanation had an impact on Amy. She imagined how great it would feel not to be overextended. They had so many things to buy for their future life together. She wanted a family and didn't want to have to worry about entering that phase of her life in crushing debt. She was willing to come up with a spending plan, talk to David about it, and give it a try.

"Thanks for the idea, Ally. I'll start a list and let you know how it works out."

WHETHER YOU WENT TO COLLEGE OR NOT

Ally spent time with relatives over the Christmas holidays. On New Year's Eve, a cousin held a party where she saw some friends of the family. One of the guys, Gabe, was about Ally's age. She caught up with him for a little while and realized he didn't have much direction. He was working at the same place where he started when he was in high school. He was never interested in college. His job sounded uninspiring with no opportunities for advancement. Although it was hard to tell, he seemed content but more like he was settling because he didn't know how to change his path. It made Ally wonder if he felt disappointment. She didn't want to ask any embarrassing questions, but walked away with another topic to discuss with Victoria.

"What kind of advice do you have for people who didn't go to college?" Ally asked.

"A common misconception is that financial security only works for "suits," corporate executives. But people with the ability to work and a skill set can make what they want of their life. Anyone can learn a trade and develop marketable skills. Just because you don't have a college education doesn't mean that you can't be financially secure. In fact, service businesses may be more lucrative than white collar jobs. Many trades are built on skills that are not learned in college. Many entrepreneurs don't have a college education, but they have a marketable skill and business acumen.

"Millionaires are made everywhere, every day, from working hard at service businesses for which they have honed their trade. Look at flooring companies, auto collision shops, and carpenters. Civil service workers can obtain financial security if they are diligent about managing their money.

"The sales field is a great outlet for people who don't have an interest in school. Many people draw on their personality traits to develop a steady, growing clientele. Real estate sales and auto sales are two examples of careers that have provided lucrative incomes to those who apply skills to jobs that match their talents."

"I just spoke with someone who seemed to have no opportunities for advancement. It was like he was stuck with whatever measly raise his company would dole out," Ally said.

"Each person needs to find his or her gift and build on it. It may or may not include a college education. All the same methods of saving, discipline, and planning apply—it's not only for people with college degrees."

"That's good to hear. I'll pass that on to some friends who think they'll never have a comfortable life because they don't have a high-paying job."

"They are really selling themselves short. Everyone has the potential to make a better life. It's a matter of educating yourself and finding your talents, then setting a plan into motion. This country offers an infinite amount of opportunities."

A LITTLE HELP FROM FRIENDS

Ally had a rough week and needed a change of pace. The weather was bad so Ally decided to take a walk in the mall. Ally passed her favorite boutique. *I'll just go in and browse; I've been good so far and it doesn't cost anything to look.*

Ally walked around and simply looked. It had been a long time since she spent freely. The store had new spring merchandise. *Nice*, she thought as she looked at an animal-print top. She was answering the call of the wild again. *Only forty-nine dollars. Hmmm. And this really nice jacket to go with it— two hundred fifty-nine dollars.* I haven't bought myself anything in the longest time. *Maybe, just now, once.*

Remembering the pact she had with Amy, she thought she had better send a text and fast.

Hey Amy. In store. SOS.

A few minutes went by. Then her text icon popped up.

Where R U?

Mall.

Are you buying? Leave now.

But it's a cool jacket.

U don't need it.

I know.

Leave now. U will thk me later.

Can I call you?

Yes.

Ally put the pricey garments down and went outside to call Amy.

"Amy, thanks for being around."

"It sounds like I caught you just in time. What were you buying?"

"A really nice animal-print top. And a jacket."

"How much?"

"About three hundred in total."

"No way. You can certainly get something cheaper elsewhere or it will eventually go on sale. Leave now."

"I know I should leave, but…"

"Let it go. Whatever you need to buy for yourself will be there after you have paid down all your credit card debt. How did you wind up there anyway? You were really doing well avoiding the stores."

"I had a rough week and came to the mall for a walk."

"Maybe that's not the best walking trail for you. Try some yoga stretching at home if you need to do something."

"I know, but the weather's depressing today and I needed to get out."

"I get it, but leave now and go to a Starbucks. Get yourself a hot drink and give yourself credit for calling your lifeline before you blew your budget."

"OK, I'm leaving. Thanks for being there for me."

"No problem, see you on Monday."

THINKING AHEAD

The brutal winter weather was over. The temperature was getting milder. It had been nine months and Ally had made more progress than she thought possible. She really wanted to think ahead now.

"How do I make sure that I never end up in deep debt again?" she asked Victoria at their next meeting. Now that she had paid off a good chunk of her credit card debt, she wanted to make sure that she wouldn't ever have a big burden again.

"That's a great question. You do this by taking measures to protect yourself. The most common reason people wind up in bankruptcy or deep in debt is unexpected events. These are typically of a catastrophic nature, such as a medical emergency, serious illness, or a sudden job loss."

"How can I make sure those circumstances don't financially devastate me?"

"You want to make sure that you won't have to use a line of credit or a loan to cover costs due to a disastrous situation. You can help yourself by obtaining the right insurance. Make sure that you have adequate medical coverage at all times of your life.

"In addition to medical insurance, make sure that you have adequate disability insurance."

"What is disability insurance for?"

"Disability insurance is actually more important than life insurance."

"Really? Why's that?"

"You have a higher risk of being injured in your life than of actually dying. Your income-earning ability could be interrupted for a very long period of time. Disability insurance covers your monthly income while you are injured. Your employer may only cover your salary for a limited amount of time and it may not even be your full salary. Many employers do not offer a short- or long-term disability policy. Find out what your employer offers. You could possibly lose your job and not be able to find another job until fully recovered. Therefore, you may need to obtain your own private policy. You would not want to resort to using credit cards to cover your monthly living expenses.

"Other than an illness or injury, emergency situations may require large expenses. It's best to keep in mind that things break and accidents happen. They will most likely happen when you least expect it. If you have adequate insurance and savings to cover out-of-pocket expenses, you will not have to resort to credit card debt or loans to pull you through."

Ally remembered another real-life situation. "Some of my friends have had to pay for their car repairs with their credit cards. Now, they're deep in debt."

"Exactly my point. By the way, do you have renter's insurance?"

"No."

"What's the first phone call you're going to make tomorrow?"

"An insurance company, for a renter's insurance policy."

"What's the second thing you're going to do?"

"Make sure that I have adequate disability insurance."

"You got it now."

Ally envisioned reaching the level of obtaining wealth and having to carefully safeguard it. It seemed to be a better problem than the one she had now, digging out of debt. Based on Victoria's information, she would have to be as diligent in protecting wealth as she was now building toward it.

"I don't want to get too deep into money issues that you'll have in the future but, basically, make sure you have all the bases covered: retirement, investments, and insurance—life and disability. Monitor growth and safeguard assets and annuities. Everyone has adversities, so plan on having a few. Then they won't be so devastating. Always have options. Do what you can today so you have something to fall back on tomorrow."

"Even though I don't have to think about these issues today, it's good to know what will follow. What other considerations evolve from having wealth and keeping it?"

"Keep reading and learning how to answer financial questions such as the following:

- How would an increase in the interest rate affect your personal finances?
- How does the inflation rate affect your investment returns?

"Also, find streams of income. As you become more advanced in your career, you can use your skills to generate income throughout your life. Income-earning skills are currency. You can create your own currency by leveraging your knowledge into becoming an instructor or writing a book. If you have entrepreneurial skills, you can start a small side business. Constantly reinvent your life. You are ever-changing so there's no need to stay the same course year after year. Never stop learning about yourself or your career."

LIFE SKILLS

Victoria offered Ally a seat in her usual place, but did not wait for Ally to begin.

"At this point, Ally, I'd like to talk about a topic of the utmost importance. It may be critical in determining your future successes."

Ally placed her notebook on the table and gave Victoria her full attention.

"I think I've left out a key life skill: persistence. Persistence is the key to life. In several studies, it was proven that a child's success is significantly tied to character, grit, and tenacity. These studies debunked the myth that children in lower-income households can never be successful. Not true. They discovered that nurturing was important to confidence levels but if children demonstrated discipline, determination, and endurance, they reached their goals. Many things in life require stamina. The ability to demonstrate stamina is an indication that one sees a goal or obligation through to the end. These are people who don't take 'No' for an answer. Many people give up on goals way too soon.

"I just read an article on the CEO of Alibaba, Jack Ma. Jack Ma was rejected at many things in his life before Alibaba was even started. He took the entrance exam to attend college in

China three times and failed each time. He applied for thirty jobs and was rejected. He applied to the police department and was rejected. He even applied at a Kentucky Fried Chicken, one of twenty-four applicants. The other twenty-three were hired. Did he stop moving ahead with his life? No. He went on to develop a small Internet-based business in his apartment and is currently worth twenty billion dollars."

"He didn't give up, did he?" Ally said.

"Not at all. Am I saying that you should define yourself by how many billions you have? No. But I am pointing out that you should never let anyone or anything stand in your way. No matter how many times you fail or become discouraged, you have to keep moving forward."

"I like hearing your stories. What other examples are there?"

"How about if you didn't pass an exam on the first attempt or didn't get promoted when you thought you would? That's OK. Take the exam again. Reinvent yourself. Keep learning. Stay on and wait another year for the promotion. You waited another year and didn't get the promotion? Promote yourself. Find another employer, one who will give you the position and salary you want. If you persist, it will come. More success stories have depended on persistence than on any other personality trait. Some people achieve success the first time around with everything they strive for. Some don't. Never give up on yourself. If you improve on your skills, no one can deny that you deserve the position that you want, or the compensation you're requesting.

"This is what Calvin Coolidge said:

> Nothing in the world can take the place of Persistence. Talent will not; nothing is more common than unsuccessful men with talent. Genius will not; unrewarded genius is almost a proverb. Education will not; the world is full of educated derelicts. Persistence and determination alone are omnipotent. The slogan 'Press On' has solved and always will solve the problems of the human race.

"So, it's not all about being smart, is it?"

"That's correct. Being smart doesn't always mean being motivated. Another quality is the sister to persistence: tenacity. Tenacity means accepting failure and moving forward anyway. Tenacity means that you go the distance when others fall behind. You hear 'No' several times a day? Find a way to 'Yes.' Stretch your imagination to find new solutions. This happens when you keep your goals in the forefront of your mind.

"I know many people who were derailed by the economic downturn of 2008. Careers needed rebuilding or restarting, net worth needed to be regained."

"That was a tough time for many people, wasn't it? I'll bet they had to call on their tenacity to recover," Ally added.

"Absolutely. The success stories of the world are a result of persistence and tenacity. Successful people anticipate failures, bumps in the road, and obstacles. Use instances of failure as a moment to recognize poor timing or the need for an alternate method. Take your time and take breaks if necessary, but don't stop. If you need to reflect and do some research, that's OK.

"If you have set a goal, don't abandon it because of difficulty. Big goals aren't achieved without some level of struggle. Ask any entrepreneur. I recommend you read some biographies of entrepreneurs who began with nothing and built empires.

"Avoid people who are negative and stay loyal to your goals. Find supporters. Reach out to different people if you have exhausted your resources."

Ally's new mantra would be "Don't Give Up."

TAKING CHARGE OF YOUR HEALTH

Ally and Victoria both realized that Ally had grown so much from the mentoring sessions that she was able to move forward on her own. In one of their last sessions, Victoria had one other important point to make.

"Let me give you my final small, but invaluable, piece of information. It may sound unrelated to financial success, but trust me, it is equally as important as all the other concepts we've discussed.

"You must take charge of your health. One of the first accomplishments of my life was taking care of my health. Health is wealth. You will not be able to accomplish what you wish for if you are sick or have a fuzzy mind. You will need to work long hours and will be no help to your employer if you're always tired. Read books about health and nutrition, eat healthy foods, and exercise.

"I didn't learn healthy habits from my family. My own mother died at a fairly young age due to her poor health habits. She was overweight and sickly most of her adult life. She relied on doctors to manage her health. Don't let anyone—not even a doctor—be in control of your health. You know how you feel. Take control of your health now. Recognize that it's not normal to be sick all the time. Unless it's absolutely necessary, don't accept a blanket diagnosis or fall into a habit of taking prescription drugs every day of your life.

"Illnesses are expensive. I had a friend who needed six hundred dollars out of pocket each month to cover her prescription medications. Being sick will cost you in days missed at work as well as the cost of the medications. Medical insurance doesn't cover everything and you will have to pay out-of-pocket expenses. The healthier you are, the less you will have to spend. Recognize that your time is valuable. Don't waste your valuable time being ill. Taking charge of your health is key to advancing in life.

"Are you aware of all the ways that poor health will disrupt your progress?"

"I never really thought about it, and am interested in every bit of advice you have for me."

"If you constantly call in sick, your manager will never be able to rely on you to travel and visit clients, your superiors may never rely on you to give presentations. You may never be referred for projects outside your routine work. Finally, you might not be referred for a promotion."

"I didn't take all that into consideration, but I will now." Ally was astonished that responsibility for one's health could be integrated into a financial lesson. It did make her think of the time that she missed three days one week and then two the next when her group's big presentation was due. Her manager was really disappointed with her for missing so much time. It was also a missed opportunity for being able to gain experience with a big project. That could have been her chance to showcase her skills or at least demonstrate her dedication to her department's efforts.

In any case, Ally had never heard financial advice that was related to her health. She sat at the edge of her chair, taking notes. Victoria was, once again, giving captivating advice and it made perfect sense. Each and every person must possess a clear mind and be as healthy as possible to be valuable to an employer or a business venture. All of us have responsibility for our own health and must respect ourselves enough to take good care of our physical and psychological well-being. What good is a tired, lethargic person? One can never succeed in life weighed down by a sluggish body. One needs energy to have accomplishments and learn skills.

"Feed your body healthy food, get enough rest, make exercise a priority, and your body will help you accomplish your goals. Your body is your vehicle on the path of success. Energy equals accomplishments."

Ally mentioned that she had been bringing healthy lunches to work for several months now and it really did make a difference.

"I also want to bring to your attention that increasing health-care costs are the leading cause of income inequality in America today. What it means is, if health-care insurance premiums or health-care costs increase by three percent, it will have more of an impact on someone earning a low wage than someone earning two hundred fifty thousand dollars a year. Wages have not increased at the same rate as medical-care costs. So, low-income workers have more of their income eaten up by the increasing cost of medical coverage.

"In the past, some individuals chose to opt out completely and go without medical insurance. That's the worst scenario. Medical catastrophes are one of the major reasons for bankruptcy. Now, all individuals are required to have minimal medical insurance coverage under Obamacare, which helps provide affordable health insurance. But a financial risk still exists. The cost of deductibles and portions of procedures that the individual is responsible for can quickly add up and be financially devastating.

"Medical insurance costs are usually buried in one's net pay and people forget about it as they move on with their life. Unfortunately, medical-care costs and premiums have been a huge burden for large and small businesses. When business owners don't want to bear more of the burden, they pass the cost onto their employees."

"I never really thought about it that way. Maybe I'll switch over to a Health Savings Account (HSA). Being that I don't get sick much, I can build up the money in that account and carry it forward each year. If I manage my health, I will have a large sum saved in the event of a catastrophic accident or illness."

"That's the way to go. The Health Savings Account will allow you to manage your health-care costs more effectively. You will also build up the amount of the account each year with your contributions. You keep the amount that you contribute from year to year."

"I know," Ally said. "With regular medical insurance, you pay the premium each month. If you don't get sick, it's insurance coverage money that you don't get back."

"That's right. As you build up the balance of an HSA, you are able to plan for the cost of medical procedures you may need later in life."

"I'll look into which medical providers my employer will allow me to contribute to."

"Ally, everyone worries about money, not just young, broke college grads."

"Really? Most older people seem so established and have everything under control."

"They may or may not. They also have to contain their spending the same as you. Some of them have made some serious money mistakes. Some are still taking care of their children."

"That's true. I work with someone in that situation. I was shocked to hear of an established person having such issues. They needed to work much longer than they planned to."

"Really wealthy people don't have to work, if they were lucky enough to have been born into wealth or if they've managed their money so carefully, they can afford to retire early. Some people late in their working years don't want to be working anymore. They may choose to work, but of their own accord, not because of financial restrictions."

"So, how is money a source of stress for people who have a lot of it?"

"There's stress and fear about losing it now that they have it. There's stress in managing it. It usually doesn't get any easier to manage, especially in large sums. The cost of maintaining large amounts of money can be expensive. There are lawyers and accountants that have to be paid. Accounts have to be maintained, and wealth has to be distributed equitably to avoid conflict between children. Remember the money scripts that we talked about a while ago? Everyone has them. Good thing you can break out of old learned patterns, if you try."

"Yes, I started to recognize my own money scripts and had to make sure that they didn't ruin me."

"Money scripts are really difficult to change. It takes a lot of mental discipline. Usually the fears that each person grew up with dictate money habits."

"I'll bet they can be extreme."

"You bet. They turn into money disorders, like compulsive buying, pathological gambling, compulsive hoarding, workaholism, financial enabling, financial dependence, financial denial, or financial enmeshment."

"I'm glad my habits didn't run to any of those extremes."

"Yes, be glad for that. However, where you fall in the spectrum will still influence how you maintain your financial business. The real key is identifying the money scripts and being aware of when they cause you to behave in a certain way. By altering habits when you first recognize the behavior, you have reached the ultimate goal of truly being in control of your destiny by not allowing frivolous beliefs to take over."

"No joke. It took some deep thinking to recognize my habits."

"The money scripts of the truly wealthy people fall within the following beliefs:

- Save for a rainy day
- Money buys freedom
- You need to work hard
- I deserve money

"Truly wealthy people believe that they are in control of their destiny and have the ability to fix problems if they were to suffer any. They have a high level of awareness that prevents them from repeating mistakes. Typically, people who don't have this level of awareness tend to repeat mistakes over and over again, constantly sabotaging their efforts, without knowing why they end up on the short end of life."

"That's really interesting. I never thought of it that way but it's so true. And I see it around me every day."

"Did you ever know anyone who squandered a windfall? That's an extreme example but a common one. Underspenders are another classic example. Some people are so limited in thought that they can't even enjoy what they have. People with a healthy money script make effective decisions that help them find the balance in enjoying material possessions without putting their finances in jeopardy."

"Balance. That's the key isn't it?"

"Everything in life requires balance."

YOU ARE THE CEO OF YOUR LIFE

Ally was a regular at Victoria's library presentations. Victoria had developed a following and the crowd was building. Ally managed to grab two seats right up front, one for her and one for her mom.

As Victoria scanned the crowd, she noticed Gail sitting beside Ally. Victoria's eyes stopped moving and Gail waved. Victoria smiled and her mind filled with memories of their friendship. She thought of how great it was to meet new people, but it was equally as good to be surrounded by people with whom there are solid bonds.

Good morning, ladies. I'm so happy to see all of you and know that you are here because something in you tells you that you have something to learn. What you learn today may surprise you. I am here to tell you that you can achieve what you long for. Whatever it is you long for, you can materialize. The key is to link your financial skills and your life goals. What are your life goals? Do you want to take a luxurious vacation each year? Do you want to have a vacation home in the mountains? Do you want to retire early? Do you want to send all of your children to college?

Think about your life goals. Decide what you want from your life and realize that you can have it.

This is not about "The Secret." This is not about expressing gratitude and waiting for it to fall into your lap. Life rarely happens that way. You must be prepared to focus and take planned steps toward your life goals. And you will reach them.

If you don't make choices for yourself, someone will make them for you. You can be in control of your destiny and it begins with your financial position. Whether it's negotiating for a house, car, or job, you will be able to have life on your terms.

So, what does money do for you?

Money buys your lifestyle.

Money buys your security.

Money offers you choices.

Always take care of your needs first. If someone else does, it may end one day. And it will probably come with a steep price to pay.

Each person has her own version of wealth. Decide what yours is and claim it. You don't want to survive, you want to live. You deserve to live a full life.

Therefore, I wish to impress upon you that your life should be conducted as a business enterprise.

A business has its revenue and expenses as its main concern. You should be just as concerned with the revenue and expenses of your personal household. Here are the parallels. A business is concerned with bringing in the highest amount of revenue. That is the means by which all of the functions will be possible. Same with your life. If you don't work and earn an income, it won't be possible for you to have food, shelter, and clothing.

Businesses have strict expense control policies. Before a business agrees to make a purchase, its financial analysts determine the return on investment of the purchase. If the return on investment does not meet their minimum threshold, the purchase will not be approved. Expense controls are a top priority for businesses. Purchasing departments will research an expense to keep costs within a range, often with maximum amounts to be spent. These two concepts are probably the hardest for an individual to relate to. Typically, there are no rational thoughts applied when making a purchase. More importantly, there are no cost controls for expenditures. Imagine determining the return on investment when purchasing household goods such as expensive décor items or household appliances. It can be done, but is usually not for a typical household. There is most certainly a return on investment on each item, but the nature of the purchase is usually not analyzed in that manner. Individuals sometimes keep costs within their limit, sometimes not. Establish your own expense controls and stick to them.

Business expenses are broken out by category. Expenses can be fixed or variable. Household expenses can be fixed, such as a monthly mortgage payment, or they can be variable, such as sporadic leisure activities. Every household has minimum expenses to pay for the standard of living that is maintained.

The net profit, or cash flow after expenses, will determine the amount of dividends that can be paid back to the business investors. For an individual, the cash flow after expenses will determine how much can be spent on leisure activities or accumulated for future use. The cash management department of a business assists the enterprise in earning the highest return on its net cash flow. The business can invest in securities or keep cash on hand. Typically, a business will evaluate the risk associated with the investment. Many investments are applied to hedge the cost of the main product component the business utilizes in its main product. Investments are purchased with short-term cash flow needs and long-term cash flow needs in mind.

Do you see the parallels? Individuals are encouraged to make investments with their net cash flow. But first, they need to determine their risk threshold. Then, keeping cash flow needs in mind, they need to determine whether their investments should be long-term or short-term. You wouldn't invest in a rental property if you needed the money within one year to cover a large expense. You would choose a savings account or a CD account. There are so many investments out there it can be dizzying, but by educating yourself, it is possible to choose the right investment for yourself.

Most people are doing this every day to some extent without realizing it. However, expense control is usually loose and can be derailed. Insufficient information about investments or skepticism of the capital markets results in poor cash management. To really be efficient about it, attention to the business model is necessary to yield the highest level of satisfaction. Household expense control needs to be monitored just like a business model.

Business managers or CEOs would not be employed for long if they were frivolous with their business methodology. Good business managers know how to create revenue, utilize resources efficiently, control costs, and manage cash effi-

ciently. They safeguard the assets of the enterprise by controlling debt. This avoids bankruptcy by maintaining liquidity. Ultimately, they provide a return to investors.

All of these measures can be applied to your personal household. You avoid bankruptcy the same way a business does. You need to be controlling debt. If not, you are putting your assets at risk of bankruptcy. It's an equation. Income-Expenses=Profit.

To establish your plan, you must determine the standard of living that you would be most comfortable with.

You want to obtain the highest standard of living as possible, and you define your own standard.

EPILOGUE

Amy's wedding was gorgeous. So was Ally's dress, rented online for fifty dollars. The designer clothing online rental service was phenomenal. Ally thought she would have to go into debt to get an appropriate dress for the event. She also wanted to give a generous wedding gift. She managed to do both, affordably.

After devoting eighteen months to learning about financial management, Ally felt she deserved to take some time for herself and treat herself to a vacation.

She looked out the airplane window. The plane was about to land at Denver International Airport. She deserved this trip and was really excited about her vacation. It was the middle of the summer, a beautiful time to travel to Colorado. She was going to drive to Breckenridge in the Colorado Rocky Mountains, and go hiking, biking, and running. She felt such confidence in the knowledge that she gained. By now, she had been promoted and her career was at full tilt. She had thousands in the bank and was working towards a down payment on a two-story townhouse just outside the city.

Ally relished the feeling that she was in an upward spiral. Her future looked and felt much brighter now that she had a solid footing on her finances. The possibilities seemed limitless; anything could be created by taking action. Feeling financial security touched her core and added a dimension to Ally's life that hadn't seemed reachable. It was a rich way of looking at life. Her self-esteem and grace had grown in multiples.

She thought of Victoria with fondness and gratitude. Ally remembered Victoria telling her that if she stuck with it, it would happen.

BIBLIOGRAPHY

Klontz, Brad and Klontz, Ted, *Mind Over Money*, New York: Crown Publishing Group, 2009.

Klontz, Brad, *Wired For Wealth*, Deerfield Beach: HCI Books, 2008.

Marshall, Susan, *How To Grow A Backbone*, New York: McGraw Hill Professional, 2000.

Perle, Liz, *Money: A Memoir: Women, Emotions, and Cash*, New York: Henry Holt and Co., 2006.

Rose, Charlie, "Charlie Rose Talks to Jack Ma", *Bloomberg Businessweek*, page 36, January 29, 2015.

Sullivan, Paul, *The Thin Green Line*, New York: Simon & Schuster, 2015.

Tough, Paul, *How Children Succeed: Grit, Curiosity, and the Hidden Power of Character*, New York: Houghton Mifflin Harcourt, 2012.

Wilson, Jennifer, “The leadership cycle: The parallel paths of career and firm success”, *Journal of Accountancy*, June 1, 2013, journalofaccountancy.com/issues/2013/jun/20137148.html.

ONLINE REFERENCES

annualcreditreport.com
bankrate.com
credit.com
creditkarma.com
dripadvice.com
equifax.com
experian.com
mint.com
moneymanagement.org
msn.com/en-us/money
investopedia.com
transunion.com

INDEX

Made in the USA
Monee, IL
04 November 2026

67374658R00108